Suffer the Children

—— ઙ∾ ——

A Theology of Liberation by a Victim of Child Abuse

JANET PAIS

Paulist Press
New York/Mahwah

Library of Congress Cataloging-in-Publication Data

Pais, Janet, 1944–
  Suffer the children: a theology of liberation by a victim of child abuse/Janet Pais.
      p.   cm.
  Includes bibliographical references and index.
  ISBN 0-8091-3226-5
  1. Children (Christian theology).   2. Image of God.   3. Child abuse—Religious aspects—Christianity.   4. Abused children—Religious life.   5. Adult child abuse victims—Religious life.   6. Pais, Janet, 1944–   . I. Title.
  BT705.P35   1990
  261.8'3423—dc20   90-25365
                                                                          CIP

Published by Paulist Press
997 Macarthur Boulevard
Mahwah, New Jersey 07430

Printed and bound in the
United States of America

Contents

Introduction

No statement, theological or otherwise, should be made that
would not be credible in the presence of burning children.[1]

Rabbi Irving Greenberg made this statement while reflecting on
the deaths of a million and a half Jewish children in the holocaust.[2]
Acts of genocide still occur in the world. And today in the United
States we are increasingly aware of other forms of attacks on children,
attacks that go on daily in our neighborhoods and even in our homes.
In alarming numbers, adults, a large percentage of whom were themselves abused as children, batter children and abuse them sexually,
emotionally, and psychologically.

Victims of the various forms of child abuse have begun speaking
out, and I believe it is time for our voices to join those of other
oppressed peoples in the attempt to articulate a theology of liberation
for our group and for all humankind. This is the theology of God the
Child. When we abuse a child, we abuse God's creation; we abuse
Godself. I offer this theology for the liberation of all abused children,
both the little and the not so little ones who are now being abused,
and those children and adults who carry the scars of childhood abuse
and all too often pass them on to the next generation. This theology is
also for all people who care about children and would like to do
something about child abuse. Child abuse affects all of us, and we all
share responsibility for an attitude toward children that makes child
abuse possible.

I refer to myself and others as "victims" of child abuse, but
"victim" is not our identity. We need for you to see who we really are,

1

to know our value as human beings, to treasure our gifts, to appreciate our courage. Like you, we are both strong and weak, both powerful and powerless, both needy and abundantly gifted. Do not feel sorry for us. Have respect for us. Enter into real relationship with us. Do something about the attitudes and abuses that force us to speak as "victims" of child abuse.

In this book I seek to address the theological issues that are relevant to adult attitudes toward children and to their relationships with children. Chapter 1 reviews the problems affecting children that are all too apparent in our culture and asserts that "the problem" is not the children. The problem stems from a widespread adult atti- tude of contempt for children because of their relative smallness, weakness, and neediness. Contempt creates an atmosphere in which abuse can happen. It results in the adult-child split, an outer split between adults and children and an inner split with the adult's own inner child-self. Contempt forces the rejection of childhood feelings and perceptions of reality and makes empathy with children impossible.

Chapter 2 explains why this is a theology of liberation and why I and other adults who were victims of childhood abuse can and must speak on behalf of the children. Here I draw the connection between my personal experiences and the development of this theology, and I also show the relevance of this theology to all adults.

Chapters 3 through 6 look at various adult attitudes toward children and explore the possibility of moving past attitudes to true relationship with children, including our inner child-selves. Chapter 3 considers relationship with the child through the eyes of Mary and Joseph and shows that Jesus taught us to see in every child received in his name the new creation, Christ himself, God the Child incarnate. Chapter 4 explores interpretations of the doctrines of the fall and original sin, in light of the adult-child split and the understanding of the child developed in Chapter 3, in an effort to move past attitudes about good and evil in children that are obstacles to true relationship and that may contribute to abuse. Chapter 5 shows how certain attitudes about good and evil in children, and specifically in their feelings, have sometimes amounted to religious rationalizations for abuse. Chapter 6 looks at sexual and aggressive feelings from certain psychoanalytic and psychological points of view, and from my personal point of view, which reflects my experiences of sexual abuse and my aggressive feelings toward my abuser. This chapter considers the reactive nature of aggression in the abused person and looks at issues concerning human responsibility for aggression.

In addition to the supposed evil of children, as evidenced by their aggression, a further rationalization for abuse may lie in the idea that human fathers follow the model of God the Father in punishing disobedience and molding children to be good. Therefore, Chapters 7 through 10 focus on attitudes about "God the Father." The gospel reveals the divine Father-Son relationship as a model, not of authoritarian punitiveness, but of adult-child relationship based on mutuality, respect, unity, and wholeness, as Chapter 7 shows. Chapter 8 considers certain attitudes about "God the Father" that are based on human experiences of authoritarian fathers. The authoritarian model feeds into the attitudes about adults and children that perpetuate the adult-child split. Chapter 9 looks at the idea that God is wrathful because of human sinfulness and explores a possible way of understanding God's wrath, not as the anger of an authoritarian father toward disobedient children, but as the anger of a child who is subject to contempt and abuse and whose God-given wholeness is broken as the adult-child split is passed on from generation to generation. Chapter 10 shows, through an analysis of symbol creation and projection, how the incarnation bridges the gap between an idea of "God" based on the projection of experiences of authoritarian human fatherhood and the Father whom the gospel reveals in the Father-Child relationship. The incarnation responds to and transforms human ideas of fatherhood that cause adult-child splits and are obstructive of true relationship. Chapters 8 and 10 also explore why we must deal with the idea of God as "Father" and must not simply dispense with the masculine label as a sexist projection.

Chapters 11 and 12 relate the gospel message to the issues of inner healing and forgiveness. Child abuse can end only when adults heal their inner adult-child splits and become capable of empathy and true relationship with children. Chapter 11 shows how the emerging wholeness of the inner child-self can heal the split in the adult and how the crucifixion and resurrection serve as a model for inner healing. Chapter 12, drawing heavily on my personal experience, considers the commandment to honor father and mother in the context of contempt and abuse, and explores whether, and how, forgiving one's abuser may be possible.

Chapter 13 attempts to sketch what a true adult-child relationship might look like, taking into account what we have learned from the relationships of Mary and Joseph to Jesus, of God the Father to God the Child, and of human adult to inner child-self. This chapter also explores the meaning and the importance of true relationship.

Chapter 14 suggests some ways in which the church and the parish community can implement the theology for the liberation of children. This final chapter includes as examples a brief homily appropriate for children and a lengthier scriptural reflection for adults.

I wish to express my thanks to Professor Ann Belford Ulanov of the department of psychiatry and religion at Union Theological Seminary for advising me on the thesis from which this book grew; to Union Theological Seminary for the excellent and stimulating education that I received there, and especially for the award of the Travelling Fellowship, which enabled me to travel and to complete work on the manuscript for this book; to Janet L. Willen, Fr. William D. Larkin, C.S.P., Fr. Frank Desiano, C.S.P., Fr. Richard Colgan, C.S.P., and my editor, Georgia Christo, for their thoughtful comments and loving encouragement; and to my husband and to the parish community of the Church of St. Paul the Apostle, for helping to give me new life.

CHAPTER 1

The Adult-Child Split: An "Attitude Problem"

THE PROBLEM OF CHILDREN

In the United States today it is easy to point out what we perceive to be "the problem of children." The news media are filled with accounts of child abuse. Television talk shows regularly feature interviews with victims of child abuse, some of whom have themselves become abusing parents. We hear of adults who throw children out windows, beat them to death, plunge them into scalding water, abandon them in trash containers, use them for their own sexual gratification, or exploit them sexually for financial gain. We are all too conscious of news accounts of child-murder or cases of abuse and neglect that have led to the deaths of children. We may be less conscious of the devastating effects of psychological or emotional abuse, such as the narcissistic wounding inflicted by adults who shame and humiliate children and tell them that they are stupid, inept, lazy, immoral, good-for-nothing, worthless, cannot do anything right, or will never amount to anything. We are just beginning to develop a consciousness about systematic attacks on the self-esteem of many children, although if we listen we can hear such attacks going on all around us. We can only guess at the numbers of children who are victims of the various forms of abuse.

At the same time as we are becoming more conscious of child abuse, our society appears superficially to be child-centered. Consumer goods aimed at the childhood market abound, and parenthood has come back into fashion among young urban professionals. Rich or poor, adults seem to see their offspring as objects to be controlled and molded into obedient, respectful children, and later into successful, prosperous citizens. Some parents begin to plan their children's academic careers at birth, and many seem to value academic achievements more highly than any other aspect of childhood.

With all this marketing, molding, and educating, how much do we adults really care about the children themselves, their feelings and their perceptions of reality? The care of children is more and more often left to persons other than their parents, persons who may or may not be competent in child care or really care about the children. In some cases, substitute caregivers may actually do a better job of child rearing than the parents would do, but it is extremely rare that a person outside the family can give a child the necessary feeling of being someone special, someone truly valued. To a child, the parents' absence says far more eloquently than any words that they do not value their child enough to spend time with the child. A young child cannot understand adult reasons, and the message of absence may be equally devastating to the child when the parents are not absent by choice. Even with the best of substitute care, continuity is at risk, and for many parents adequate substitute caregivers simply are not available. There are crises of child care for the children of working parents and of foster care for children who cannot live at home. Persons employed in animal care often receive higher wages than those who care for children. Homemakers, whether female or male, are almost always unpaid and without prestige (and thus narcissistically wounded) in our money-conscious society. Sheer need, as well as the competitive priorities of our economic system, reduces the possibilities for parents who care deeply about their children to have "spare" time to spend with them. Many children are relegated to hobby or even nuisance status. As a society, we clearly have not placed the real needs of children very high on our list of priorities.

Still, in many cases, the project of molding children appears to work well until adolescence, when adults begin, if they have not already done so, to perceive the children as "the problem." Adults feel that they have done their best, have given their children every-thing, yet all around them they see teenage drug and alcohol abuse.

Many teens run away from home, engage in prostitution rather than return home, commit violence, commit suicide. Indeed, some parents have thrown out their teenaged children, who then have no homes to return to. In addition, teenaged children in alarming numbers are having children of their own for whom they cannot adequately care.

Meanwhile, the evidence mounts indicating that abusing parents usually were themselves victims of abuse as children. The cycle of violence directed inward and outward seems unbreakable. Children are starved, beaten, raped, humiliated, manipulated, lied to. And child-related problems exist within a larger context of world violence, terrorism, substance abuse, poverty, oppression, homelessness, hunger, racism, sexism, environmental pollution, and the threat of nuclear war. We grown-up children, with our contempt for God's creation, threaten ourselves with the destruction of human existence as we know it.

"THE PROBLEM" IS NOT THE CHILDREN

Just as "the problem" of racism or sexism or poverty does not reside in the person who is black or female or economically disadvantaged, "the problem" of children does not reside in children. The problem is an adult problem, and in particular a problem stemming from the attitude of many adults toward children. The problem begins with an attitude toward children that is far more subtle and pervasive than we might expect. In fact, to some extent, this attitude probably affects every child, and therefore every one of us. This attitude is contempt.

Swiss psychoanalyst and writer Alice Miller provides the following example of adult contempt for the child that illustrates the ordinariness and ubiquity of this attitude:

> I was out for a walk and noticed a young couple a few steps ahead, both tall; they had a little boy with them, about two years old, who was running alongside and whining. . . . The two had just bought themselves ice-cream bars on sticks from the kiosk and

were licking them with enjoyment. The little boy wanted one, too. His mother said affectionately, "Look, you can have a bite of mine, a whole one is too cold for you." The child did not want just one bite but held out his hand for the whole ice, which his mother took out of his reach again. He cried in despair, and soon exactly the same thing was repeated with his father: "There you are, my pet," said his father affectionately, "you can have a bite of mine." "No, no," cried the child and ran ahead again, trying to distract himself. Soon he came back again and gazed enviously and sadly up at the two grown-ups, who were enjoying their ice creams contentedly and at one. Time and again he held out his little hand for the whole ice-cream bar, but the adult hand with its treasure was withdrawn again.

The more the child cried, the more it amused his parents. It made them laugh a lot and they hoped to humor him along with their laughter, too. . . . When his father had completely finished his ice cream, he gave the stick to the child and walked on. The little boy licked the bit of wood expectantly, looked at it, threw it away, wanted to pick it up again but did not do so, and a deep sob of loneliness and disappointment shook his small body. Then he trotted obediently after his parents.[1]

Miller points out that these parents frustrated their son's legitimate narcissistic needs and thus wounded him when they made fun of his wish for an ice-cream bar of his own. They belittled his wishes and his disappointment. It was not the ice cream that he needed so much as the recognition it would imply that he was a person too, deserving of respect. His parents did not take his feelings or his needs seriously.[2]

Miller suggests that the pervasive and usually (by adults, at least) unnoticed contempt that these parents exhibited is at bottom adult contempt for human weakness and need, in children and in adults themselves. Having experienced the humiliation that goes with receiving such contempt as children, adults need to reassure them-selves that they are strong and powerful, usually at the expense of someone smaller or weaker, such as a child.[3] They do not ever want to feel small and powerless again, as they did as children, and so they deny the importance of such feelings in their child.

In rejecting the weakness, neediness, and humiliations of their own childhoods, adults split their conscious sense of who they are as adults both from their inner experience of being a child—their child-selves—and from the children they encounter in the world. The inner child-self is the presently existing reality of the experience each of us had of being a child, an experience that is stored in us in memories and even more vividly in patterns of feelings, many of them repressed. The child who once felt those feelings remains, however, a living reality of whom we can become aware through feelings, attitudes, and behaviors that sometimes arise from the unconscious mind and that we, as adults, cannot fully understand or control. Adults try to keep this child-self under control by keeping it out of consciousness, or by admitting the child only as something foreign to the adult-self.

The effect of this inner adult-child split is an implicit assumption that children are somehow fundamentally different from adults, and the difference translates as inferiority. Adults define themselves as strong, children as weak, and adults have no use for weakness. For the adult, the child embodies what the adult has inwardly rejected, and usually repressed, primarily because of the contempt and humiliation suffered in the adult's own childhood.

An example may help to clarify the nature of the inner adult-child split. A woman in a church discussion group related: "I have recently become aware that what seem like my needs, but are not really, are directed by a part of me that is not really me. It is like a little person inside of me who demands all kinds of attention. With the help of prayer, I am making a lot of progress with overcoming this person. I guess it has been with me since childhood." Later she referred to this "little person" as "the little monster." She related this in connection with a discussion of temptation to sin. She experienced her child-self as something sinful and self-willed, and she was not willing to accept it as part of who she really is.

Most adults are not conscious of their child-selves, having repressed or split off their unwanted childhood feelings and perceptions of reality. The first step toward regaining the wholeness that existed prior to the adult-child split is to become conscious of those childhood feelings and connect them with their childhood origins. The woman in the church discussion group had made important progress in be-coming conscious of the existence of her child-self, but she failed to recognize its true significance and was determined to maintain the inner adult-child split, if possible by repressing once more her child-self's unwanted feelings and needs. The next step toward wholeness would be to begin to take her child-self with all the unwanted feelings and needs seriously. Instead, adults who suffered contempt in child-hood have contempt for the smallness, weakness, and neediness of their child-selves and of children.

Contempt is the pollution of our human environment. Like much of the poison in the air we breathe, contempt is usually invisible to us. Having contempt means that our behavior toward the smaller, weaker, needier person is different from the way we would behave toward the same person if she or he were as big and strong as we are. It means taking advantage in some way, or playing on the smallness, weakness and neediness of the child. We say that children should be seen and not heard. We say that children don't feel things the way we adults do, imagining that adults feel more deeply than children. We say to a child, "Don't be a baby," thus at the same time expressing our contempt for the child and teaching the child to have contempt for anyone who is smaller and weaker. We say that "childish" is not the same as "childlike," the one undesirable, the other desirable. This is an expression of contempt for the child's point of view. We say, "Don't be a child!" Jesus tells us the opposite: Be a child! Be the child you were and still are, the child-self who is still alive in you.

Widespread contempt for small, weak, needful children is an attitude that underlies the various forms of physical, sexual, and psy-chological/emotional abuse. The contemptuous adult views the ob-ject of contempt indeed as an object, not as a person worthy of re-spect. Contempt itself thus is abusive and oppressive. Adults, often unconsciously, act toward children out of an attitude that the child is a possession properly subject to their control. Because adults have power over children, too often they use it, not for the true good of the child, but just to "show who is the boss." Every act of child abuse is also an abuse of power, and every abuse of power necessarily implies contempt for the less powerful person.

An adult may value a child for what the child can do or achieve, but this is not the same as valuing the child simply for being who and what the child is. With a contemptuous attitude, an adult may use a child for the adult's own purposes, mold the child to be what the adult wants the child to be, or identify the child as the source of problems or feelings that in fact belong to the adult. With contempt for a child's feelings, an adult may ridicule and humiliate the child, threaten or injure the child physically, or use the child sexually. Battering and sexual abuse also reflect a lack of respect for the child's bodily integrity.

With contempt for a child's perceptions of reality, an adult may lie to or manipulate the child or force the child to deny his or her own feelings or perceptions. An adult may fail to trust a child, explicitly accuse the child of lying, or implicitly lack respect for the child's word. The adult may tell the child she or he does not really feel the way the child says she or he feels. For example, as a child I hated my younger brother, but my parents told me repeatedly, "You don't hate your brother. You love him. You'll laugh about this someday." I am not amused, either by the fact that I hated my brother or by my parents' denial of my feelings. This was not the most damaging instance of their denial, however, because my feeling of hatred for my brother was one that I was able to hold consciously and articulate. I suspect that this was true because, in their contempt for my brother's feelings, my parents did not find my hatred for him seriously threatening, as they would have found my hatred for either of them. I had to repress all my hostile feelings toward my parents and my older sister. I was free to hate my brother simply because he was the only family member smaller and (at least in his infancy) weaker than I. Contempt is passed along very early in life.

Failing to understand a child's perceptions of reality, an adult may belittle feelings that flow from those perceptions. When I was three years old I had to be hospitalized for a tonsillectomy. The night before the operation I was terrified, and my father stayed up with me all night, trying to calm me by telling me that it would not hurt. He lied. And I felt deeply betrayed when he failed to keep his promise to stay with me through the operation, a promise he knew he would not keep. He did not realize that his dishonesty mattered; after all, I was only a child. Recently, facing hospitalization again in terror, I remembered one of the reasons that I was so frightened then. I entered the hospital two months after my brother's birth. My father clearly preferred my brother, simply because he was a boy. However flawed my father's relationship with me may have been before then, it must have seemed better than the lack of relationship that ensued. I no longer existed for him. I was only a girl. My parents had gone to the hospital to get my brother, and I believed that they were taking me to the hospital to send me back. On at least one earlier occasion they had left me behind without adequate explanation—how can a two year old understand that her parents are choosing to go away with her sister and not her? I had felt abandoned, and I lived with a deep fear of abandonment. Thus, from my point of view, it was quite reasonable to believe that if my father left my side at the hospital, I would never come home again. My parents did not try to find out what I feared, and if they had found out, they probably would have scoffed. Facing this old fear in connection with this new hospitalization, in adulthood, it would be tempting to tell myself that obviously as a child I had been mistaken, that there really was nothing to fear, and to try to dismiss the old fears as they emerged. In this way I would compound my parents' contempt. To respect my child-self, her feelings, and her perceptions of reality, I could only enter into those old feelings, understand how she felt and why, and take her feelings seriously. Then I was free to face surgery with adult fears.

An adult who has contempt for the needs of a child may neglect the child physically or emotionally or wound the child by failing to value the child. A child's need for attention is a legitimate need, but often adults say with contempt, "The child only wants attention. Ignore her." Or, worse yet, "Punish her." Or, "I'll give her something to cry about!" Contempt robs the child of a God-given sense of self-worth. With a lack of respect for a child's dignity as a human being, an adult may fail to take the child seriously or to accept the child as a unique individual created in the image of God.

Jesus, the divine Child incarnate, tells those to whom he comes that if they do not become like little children they will not enter the kingdom of heaven. The child we must become like is the child who already exists in us, the child-self. This child is not an archetype or an abstract ideal, or a model of innocence, purity, and sweetness, but a flesh-and-blood reality with intense feelings such as humiliation, shame, powerlessness, anger, hatred, and rage, as well as love and joy. Children in fact do not feel things the same way adults do. They feel all feelings far more intensely because they have not begun to defend themselves against their own feelings. This was true too of our inner child-selves before we rejected them by rejecting their feelings. The high value we adults place on controlling our feelings often amounts to contempt for our own feelings and needs.

Jesus came to call not the righteous, but tax collectors and prosti-tutes, those who lacked social status and for whom humiliation was a daily concrete experience. Jesus knew that their humiliation gave them access to rejected parts of themselves and thus a hope of whole-ness that was beyond the reach of those who lorded it over people weaker than themselves. Jesus turned upside down all earthly notions of status: The powerless and the oppressed are those who count. Children fall within this category—powerless, oppressed, lacking so-cial status. But the way Jesus talks about them is not exactly the same as the way he speaks of prostitutes and tax collectors. About children he says that "to such belongs the kingdom of God."[4] Such a striking statement should not be reduced to a question of social status. The child has far greater soteriological significance, as we shall see, than the mere preferred status of the oppressed would suggest. Jesus knew well that "the problem" is not the children. The child is the key to the salvation of all of us.

CHAPTER 2

A Theology of Liberation

God Is Child

All the manifestations of adult contempt for children referred to in Chapter 1 have something in common with the various forms of prejudice and oppression in the world today. We oppress others when we control, abuse, discriminate against, or otherwise take advantage of others because of their relative weakness, powerlessness, or neediness. Adults who have contempt for relative powerlessness, weakness, and neediness may abuse and oppress children, the child aspects of themselves, and/or persons of other races or ethnic groups, the economically disadvantaged, or women, the so-called weaker sex.

Movements for the liberation of the economically oppressed in Latin America and of women and blacks in North America have produced their distinctive liberation theologies. A principal insight common to the various liberation theologies is that God is on the side of the oppressed, the weak, the needy, the powerless. Exodus tells how God heard the cries of distress of Israel in Egypt and delivered the oppressed people from slavery to form a new nation. And later Jesus announced:

> The Spirit of the Lord is upon me,
> because he has anointed me to preach good news to the poor.
> He has sent me to proclaim release to the captives
> and recovering of sight to the blind,
> to set at liberty those who are oppressed,
> to proclaim the acceptable year of the Lord (Lk 4:18–19).

Just as in biblical times, the power of God will move with those who are disadvantaged and cry out for God's help in their struggles for liberation in the world today. Each group has a unique way, or set of ways, of expressing the movement of God's power on its behalf. For example, a black theologian may assert that God is black; a feminist theologian may assert that God is woman.

Following their example, this theology for the liberation of children asserts:

GOD IS CHILD.

In fact, it is this, precisely, that the gospel asserts. For at the center of the Christian faith is the belief that God the Son, or "Child," became incarnate as the Christ child. God took on all the powerlessness, weakness, and neediness of human childhood for our salvation.

In writing this book, I assert the right, which blacks, women, and the economically oppressed have claimed, to question basic assumptions of traditional interpretation that may result from and perpetuate oppressive systems. In relation to children, such assumptions might be called "adultist."

At the same time, I set myself the task of taking seriously elements of Christian tradition such as use of the "Father" image for the first person of the Trinity, the idea that God is at times angry in relation to humankind, and notions of the "fall" and of "original sin." Each of these elements can play a liberating role, but each has at times been interpreted in oppressive ways. Some men have claimed the "Father" image as an indication of divine masculinity and as a justification for an authoritarian and oppressive exercise of power over those who are weaker, including children. Seeing in the wrath of God a sign of divine paternal anger and punitiveness, some fathers have felt justified in behaving abusively toward children. Some women too have followed this misunderstood parental model. And some adults have thought that children deserve punishment and need molding to be good because of an evil, sinful nature inherited due to the fall and original sin. There are, however, ways of understanding these ele-

ments of tradition that go beyond the sometimes harmful interpretations of the past and move toward the deeper truth of the gospel of
God the Child, which requires us to place the highest value on children and to treat them with ultimate seriousness and respect.

A liberation theology in this context must be a theology that
manifests respect for the child, acknowledges the child's value, and
accepts and values all the child's feelings and perceptions of reality,
including not only the child's strengths and gifts, but also the child's
weakness and neediness, as well as the child's anger and other aggressive feelings. A theological understanding of the child and of God the
Child will enhance the possibility of a change in adult attitudes toward, and in adult relationships with, both external children encoun-
tered in the world and adults' internal child-selves.

WHO WILL SPEAK FOR THE CHILD? WHO WILL LISTEN?

Each oppressed group has found it necessary to speak for itself
and to create its own liberation theology. To the oppressed, outsiders
who attempt to speak on their behalf, however supportive their intentions, seem to have a condescending or patronizing attitude—and
these attitudes are forms of contempt. "I will help you" often translates as "I will do for you what I do not think you are capable of doing
for yourself."

The case of children as an oppressed group is unique. Children
do not have the education or the resources necessary to speak for
themselves or, having spoken, to effect any change. In fact, their
plight is worse than a lack of education or resources. An outstanding
feature of their oppression is that their feelings and perceptions of
reality are so often denied; abused children are often denied the ability
to know what is happening to them or that it could possibly be any
other way: Adults who abuse children often tell them it is for their
own good.[1] And the biblical commandment to honor father and
mother often heaps guilt on any child who somehow is able to react
against abuse, even when the child has grown to adulthood.[2]

Children are innately powerless to do anything about their oppression. The only "actions" available to children in reaction to their abuse, such as conforming to adult wishes, running away, dropping out, suicide, substance abuse, behavior problems, and mental illness, tend not to liberate children, but rather to make their oppression worse.

Unlike minority groups and the poor, children can never gain equal access to power as children. They can only grow up, out of their oppressed status, and become part of the more powerful group— adults—who oppressed them. This inevitable shift of status makes a struggle for the liberation of children all the more difficult. Since those who have been abused are more likely than others to become abusers, many abuse victims tend to take on a vested interest in upholding the point of view of the oppressors just at the time when they gain the education and resources that would enable them to speak for the oppressed. Even abusers who feel helpless and remorseful, and abuse victims who do not become child abusers, are likely to feel contemptuous of their own weaknesses and therefore feel contemptuous also of the weaknesses of others, including children. Fortunately, however, some adults who were abused in childhood are in touch with their early experiences and feelings and so are able to empathize with children.

Children are inherently disadvantaged. They form the one group whose liberation can never change this. As long as a child is a child, she or he will never have access to power or resources equal to adults. Liberation in this context therefore, most clearly of all, must be interactive between strong and weak, advantaged and disadvantaged. To be sure, the movement for black or feminist liberation, although it arises from the oppressed group, cannot reach fulfillment without the eventual transformation of the group in power—white or male. The only alternative to transformation is subjection, which merely turns the tables of power and contempt. Ideally, when transformation takes place on both sides, however, there will be no more disadvantage, or advantage, based on race or sex. In those contexts relative powerlessness is not inherent but social and economic. The movement for the liberation of children, in contrast, must originate with the advantaged, the adults, and the disadvantaged status of children can never

be erased, although its significance in relationships can be trans-
formed. *The child is the key to our salvation precisely because in the
child relative weakness and disadvantage cannot be overcome, but
must be embraced and respected.*

Adults must speak for children, but how can adults speak for
children without manifesting the contempt they seek to combat?
Scripture tells us that we are all children in God's sight, and psychology tells us that we never completely leave our childhoods behind,
that childhood experiences and feelings remain with us throughout
our lives, buried in our unconscious minds to the extent that we have
rejected them from consciousness. The child-self within every one of
us cries for a hearing, if only we would listen. The adult who is in
touch with the experiences and feelings of childhood can and must
speak for the child, speak as the child within.

Adults who were victims of abuse in childhood in particular
share the status of the abused, oppressed child. Without healing,
these adults are oppressors as well as oppressed, as they maintain
adult-child splits and oppress their inner child-selves, if not children
in the world. To the extent that they reject their own feelings of
childhood humiliation, pain, weakness, helplessness, and neediness,
they will have contempt for such feelings in children. Thus the first
liberation must be of the adult's inner child-self, who can then guide
the adult to feel empathy for all weaker and needier people, including
children, and to speak on behalf of children. This inner liberation can
lead to inner and outer healing of adult-child splits and thereby to
human liberation, wholeness, and unity.

Jesus says that we each must become "like a child" to enter the
reign of God. When the adult who was an abuse victim becomes "like
a child," like the child that adult once was, he or she can and must
speak for all abused children. Such adults must opt to identify with
abused children and thus speak in empathy with all oppressed children, rather than maintaining a preference for an adulthood contemptuous of the weakness and neediness of childhood. Paradoxically, it takes enormous strength to face and accept repressed feelings
of pain, humiliation and helplessness. The feelings of childhood are

intense, and adult contempt masks a deep and understandable fear of feeling them once again.

The oppressed child within me is crying out in pain and protest. It is she who is responsible for the writing of this book. I think of her as "LJ" (Little Janet). LJ is not a problem to be solved, but a real, hurt, human being to be lived with, related to, loved, trusted, valued, taken seriously, and respected. Living with LJ is the story and the meaning of my life—all of my life, not just my past, not a phase I have to go through and get over. It is always tempting to try to abandon her again, to repress her feelings and reinstitute the inner adult-child split. But now that I am conscious of her and in relationship with her I know that I am responsible to her and that only she can heal me, with God's help. She is God's truth within me, the power of God in creation moving for my liberation and transformation.

LJ is abused sexually, neglected emotionally, wounded narcissis-tically, and denied her feelings and her perceptions of reality. If I were to begin the preceding sentence with "I," I would probably phrase it in the past tense. But the present tense is more appropriate, because LJ has shown me that these old experiences are still alive, ongoing emotional realities underlying what I like to think of as my adult life. I have learned the vital importance of taking LJ's reality seriously, how-ever painful or inconvenient her feelings and needs may be, and how-ever inappropriate they may seem according to my adult view of things.

I was over the age of thirty when LJ introduced me to my anger, and over forty when she revealed to me feelings such as hatred for my abuser, shame, doubt, and humiliation. Before that I had continued LJ's oppression by refusing to feel such feelings—her feelings—which I had long repressed. I maintained an inner split, denying my child-self her feelings and her perceptions of reality, denying even her existence as part of me. When I first felt anger as an adult, I was not conscious of LJ, but even then the eruption of anger proved to open a way toward spiritual rebirth and creativity. My parents had not per-mitted anger. In feeling anger, which for so long I had totally rejected as part of my consciously perceived self, I became aware that I, as God created me, was more than I, as my parents had molded me, had come to be. I found gradually that my split-off and repressed aspects—expressions of LJ herself—have a force of reality that participates in the Absolute, the suchness of creation, Godself immanent.

I am writing on behalf of my child-self, LJ, not as an expert in child care, education, psychology, or theology. As an adult I have earned a B.A. in art history and French, a J.D. in law from New York University, and an M.Div. with highest honors from Union Theological Seminary in New York, with concentration in the field of psychiatry and religion. I have had varied work experience, including computer programming, Wall Street legal practice, and parish ministry. My authority does not come from my studies of psychology and theology or from my other educational or professional experience, however, but from what I share with millions of others, experiences of abuse and neglect and the struggle to find wholeness. My experiences of God and church have been integral to the healing process, and my experiences of abuse and neglect have profoundly influenced and shaped my psychological and theological understanding.

My adult training and experience make it possible for me to frame abstract theological concepts, but I seek to avoid an overly scholarly approach. I accept Robert McAfee Brown's "moral criterion for future theology: it must be a theology that puts the welfare of children above the niceties of metaphysics."[3] LJ indulges my need to engage in adult rationalizations, because she knows that I have reached even my most abstract thought through a painful effort to work out my sense of who I am, who God is, and what my relationship is with her and with God.

Who will listen to a theology for the liberation of children? I believe every adult shares responsibility for the plight of each abused child and therefore should work toward a personal theological understanding of the child. I have stated that the liberation of children must begin with adults, and specifically with the liberation of the oppressed child-selves of adults, many of whom were abuse victims as children. Adults have power over children, and the warning of the gospel is for those who have power: We are not to lord it over those

who are weaker, but to serve them. The child is Jesus' specific example of those whom we are to serve (Mk 9:33–35).

The contemptuous attitude toward smallness and weakness is
not only an attitude of individual abusive parents, but also an attitude
of society as a whole. This societal attitude unconsciously gives support to abusers in their acts of abuse and thus helps to perpetuate
abuse; society and its attitudes in turn are shaped by the broken
human products of contempt and abuse. Contempt implies narcissistic deprivation, which produces both the antisocial behavior of those
who in effect decide to be as bad as they have been told they are, and
the unhealthy competitiveness of those who strive unendingly for the
assurance, which will never really convince them, that they are, after
all, worth something. In either case the individual has an insatiable
need to feel better than someone else, to look down on someone
smaller or weaker. This contempt shapes a society that shares responsibility for all child abuse and other forms of oppression.

As Christians we must ensure that theology and religious practice support children's liberation and do not aid and abet abuse by
fostering contempt for children. We must recognize that true Christianity honors the child as a real, fully human being with value,
dignity, and integrity. The child received in Christ's name is no less
than Christ among us, to whom our ultimate duty is owed (Mk 9:37).

As a society, we must recognize how vital the issue of children's
liberation is, both in terms of the welfare of individual children and in
terms of the welfare of society as a whole. We must make children's
needs our highest priority and commit the human resources and funds
that are necessary to provide for those needs. We must stop perceiv-
ing child care as, at best, second rate work and recognize that in fact
nothing is more important. No set of problems presents a greater
challenge, and those who strive to meet this challenge deserve the
recognition and rewards due to any who undertake such a demanding
task. We need to make sure that those most capable (with the most
liberated child-selves and the greatest empathy for children) are shap-
ing child care policy and practices and caring for children. We need to
reshape our economic priorities to make it possible for caring parents

to parent, and we need to make parenting training available to all who care for children. We need to take seriously the constraints of single parent homes and homelessness among children. We need to make help readily available to those who are caught in the cycle of abuse. We must give children our best, nothing less. Respectful and loving child care must be available not only for my children and the children of my neighborhood, my race, my economic or social class, but for all children, or the cycle of violence will go on, the reign of God will continue to elude us.

CHAPTER 3

Christic and the Child:
From Attitude to Relationship

And he took a child, and put him in the midst of them; and taking
him in his arms, he said to them, "Whoever receives one such
child in my name receives me; and whoever receives me, receives
not me but him who sent me" (Mk 9:36–37).

As adults we have many attitudes about children, their feelings,
and their behavior. Even when abuse is the apparently uncontrollable
acting out of repressed rage or other reactions to abuse from an adult's
own childhood, the adult may rationalize the abuse, thinking that
"punishment" is appropriate because of evil in the child. After all,
"God the Father" punishes human beings for their disobedience, and
"he" is the model for human fatherhood, isn't "he"? And some abuse
occurs, not out of uncontrollable rage, but out of a calculated intent to
make a child be "good."[1] These attitudes about the role of adults and
the nature of children, grounded in misunderstandings of elements of
Christian tradition, can prevent adults from having the kind of relationship with children that true Christian faith demands.

Christian faith is centered on the belief that God became human
flesh in the person of the Christ child. Jesus is the Word made flesh,
God the Son (or Child) incarnate. Jesus tells us that when we receive
a child in his name we receive him, and not him, but the one who sent
him. In other words, when we receive a child in Christ's name, we
receive Christ. We receive God's creative Word in the flesh; we
receive God the Child incarnate.

In baptism we specifically receive children in Christ's name, but

23

in a broader sense, as Christians, we must receive all children in the name of Christ. Jesus himself told his disciples to let the children come to him, "for to such belongs the reign of God" (Mk 10:14). Jesus did not say that God's reign belongs only to such as baptized children, or only to such as male, or white, children. He had just been answering the questions of Pharisees, and their children were no doubt among those who approached him. Jesus received children unconditionally, and in his name we must do the same. Jesus did not receive the children so that he could lecture them on good behavior or spank them for misbehaving or making noise when he was trying to talk to other adults, but so that he could touch them in a loving, respectful, and healing way: "And he took them in his arms and blessed them, laying his hands upon them" (Mk 10:16). This is Jesus' model for relationship with children.

If we are to take seriously Jesus' words and receive each child in his name as Christ, then we must not have any attitude toward any child that would cause us to relate to that child differently from the way we would relate to the Christ child. We all share responsibility for the fate of all children. Our collective attitudes form individual attitudes (and vice versa) and limit possibilities for free relationship.

To find out more about what it would mean to receive a child in Christ's name, as Christ, let us look at the child from Mary's and Joseph's points of view. Think of Mary, visited by the angel Gabriel, who announced to her that the child to be born to her would be conceived of the Holy Spirit (Lk 1:26–35). An angel also appeared to Joseph, in a dream, telling him not to be afraid to marry Mary on account of her pregnancy, because it was of the Holy Spirit (Mt 1:18–21). Think what their attitude toward their child and his nature must have been.

Imagine having a son or daughter, knowing that the child was conceived of the Holy Spirit. You would have reverence for the child's divine origin and believe in the appropriateness of the child's nature. You would want to find out who the child is, and you would know that you could learn that only from the child. You would love and respect the child, desire to serve his or her needs, and trust the child to let you know what those needs are. You would be honored to hold and nurture the child. You would trust the child's honesty, integrity, and separate inner initiative, and have respect for his or her dignity as a human being. You would trust and respect the child's innate reactions and feelings and his or her perceptions of reality.

You would not believe that your greater age or superior physical strength or knowledge gave you the right to control, manipulate, humiliate, use, or abuse the child. Like Joseph, you would not act as if you owned the child, but you would protect the child from harm, as Joseph did[2] when he fled with Mary and Jesus to Egypt to escape Herod's massacre of male infants (Mt 2:13ff). You would not have contempt for the child's smallness, weakness or neediness. Mary let Jesus know how she felt when he stayed behind in the temple at Jerusalem when he was twelve years old, but she did not have contempt for him. Although she and Joseph did not understand his reason for staying and causing his parents so much worry, they did not abuse or humiliate him. They did not belittle his explanation, but took it, and him, seriously. Mary "kept all these things in her heart" (Lk 2:41–52).

Above all, you would trust the child to be what God intends him or her to be. You would not decide whether the child is good or evil, or think that you had to mold the child to be good. In fact, you would move beyond any "attitude" toward your child and simply relate to the child as the child is. You would be able to relax with the child. You would have faith in the child's ability to develop, just as if the child were a seed that you could trust to grow into a plant, assuming appropriate provision for needs and lack of interference. You would not presume to teach the child how to be God's Child any more than you could teach a seed how to become a plant. That is its nature.

Yes, it would all seem so clear—if your child were the Christ, the anointed one. And the world would be such a different, better place, if all children were divine in origin and perfect in human nature, if all human beings fulfilled God's intention in creating us.

Well, I have news for you. In fact, this is the good news that Jesus brought to us. Just as Gabriel announced to Mary the divine origin of Jesus, Jesus himself has announced that every child, received in his name, shares his divine identity: "Whoever receives one such child in my name receives me; and whoever receives me, receives not me but him who sent me" (Mk 9:36–37). In other words, when a Christian receives a child in the name of Christ, that child is Christ; in fact, the child is Godself. Every child received in Christ's name is thus a divine Child who "knows" how to develop into the adult God intended, just as a seed "knows" how to develop into a plant. This is the divine knowledge of God's good creation, as opposed to the demonic "knowledge concerning good and evil" that human beings have imposed on creation. God is the Creator of every child, and faith reveals the presence of the Holy Spirit in each of us and thus in the conception of each child. The angel's annunciation freed Mary and Joseph from any preconceptions and attitudes about what their child would or should be. Jesus' annunciation of your child frees you too to move beyond all attitudes to real relationship with your child as God has created him or her to be. This is, in fact, what it means to receive a child in Jesus' name, as Christ.

Christian eschatology teaches us that the reign of God, which belongs to such as the little children, is realized "already," because God has effected the "new creation" in the incarnation, crucifixion, and resurrection. But the reign of God is also "not yet"; that is, its realization remains unfulfilled, because humankind remains in a fallen, sinful state.

Adam and Eve are the human beings of the "old creation." God created Adam out of the ground, and Eve out of Adam, according to the Genesis account. Thus the old creation was the creation of adults who had never been children, adult woman from adult man. God's new creation, however, was of the child Jesus, a male infant born to a female adult, Mary, who had also been a child. Perhaps the story of Adam and Eve expresses the reason for the descent of sinfulness from generation to generation in the idea that the first parents had not been children. As parents who did not know how it felt to be children, they could hardly avoid misapprehending the nature of children, thinking children were different from, and somehow inferior to, themselves. They could hardly avoid having contempt for the relative smallness and weakness of children, causing the adult-child split in their children, and thus beginning the inevitable passage from one generation to another of brokenness and its tendency to cause more brokenness.

In the new creation God did not create adults without child-hoods. The new creation occurred through the human childhood of Godself. In the new creation God reasserted God's image in the hu-man child. By virtue of the new creation, God has let us know that it is in newborn children that the unbroken image of God is to be found.

Jesus, the Christ child, is the new creation, and every child received in Christ's name is Christ, God the Child incarnate. Every child thus is God's new creation. Every child received in Christ's name is a new creation "already," created to grow, develop, and react just as God intended. But the new creation in the child is also "not yet," as long as adults treat children with contempt and break their wholeness by causing them to reject their child-selves.

This theology for the liberation of children is inherently both practical and impractical. (See Chapter 13.) It is practical in its orien-tation toward the healing of the adult-child split. At the same time this theology is impractical, because it calls for nothing less than transformation, life according to the Spirit, entry into the reign of God. When the Galatian Christians sought rules for living, Paul re-ferred them to the "fruit of the Spirit" (Gal 5:22). The child whose spirit has not been destroyed will live by the fruit of the Spirit. Life according to the Spirit is not a predictable life, like a life according to a set of rules, however:

> The wind blows where it wills, and you hear the sound of it, but you do not know whence it comes or whither it goes; so it is with every one who is born of the Spirit (Jn 3:8).

Receiving your child in Christ's name and leaving your child free for a life in the Spirit may not be easy or convenient. It may not make you feel good; it may even be painful. But it can reverse the cycle of adult-child splits, just as the life of Jesus did. And receiving chil-dren in this manner, freeing children from the adult-child split rather than training them by contempt and abuse to be contemptuous or to be abusers in their turn, is required of us:

Whoever causes one of these little ones who believe in me to sin,
it would be better for him if a great millstone were hung round his
neck and he were thrown into the sea (Mk 9:42).

As Christians we must receive all children in Christ's name, as
the Child incarnate. We must relate to all children with the respect
due to God's new creation, as we imagine Mary must have related to
her divine Child. Mary was different from other adults. She was able
to allow Jesus to be the new creation and remain whole because she
saw the truth about what God was doing: "[H]e has scattered the
proud in the imagination of their hearts, he has put down the mighty
from their thrones, and exalted those of low degree" (Lk 1:51–52).
Mary saw that God had "regarded the low estate of his handmaiden"
(Lk 1:48); she did not take God's choice of her to mean that she
should become mighty in relation to the lowly child.

CHAPTER 4

Attitudes About Good and Evil in Children

Throughout Christian history there has been theological debate as to the nature of human beings, including children. Is the human creature good, or evil, or a combination of the two? If God is good and God's creation is good, where does evil come from? The questions and their variations go on and on, and they seem largely unanswer-able. As the theological debate has filtered through to the popular level, a great many Christian adults probably assume that the human child partakes of human sinfulness and is a mixture of good and evil. We point to the existence of aggression and self-destructiveness as evidence of the presence of evil in the world and as evidence of its effects in the child. Nevertheless, the theological debate continues, and opinions differ. Some point to the Genesis creation accounts and stress the goodness of creation. Many say that the child is good, but that the child's behavior is sometimes bad. Some even reject the idea of innate human sinfulness altogether. Philosophical, psychological, and sociological insights feed into the attitudes we form about human nature and the nature of children.

With so many different points of view confronting us, it seems that we really do not know what the nature of the child is. What we think of as the child's nature is in fact largely a matter of opinion, formed in light of our often unconscious attitudes about children. What we observe in the behavior of children is colored by what has already happened to the child, perhaps even in the womb, by what has happened to us, especially in our own childhoods, and by other preconceptions formed by the received "wisdom" of our religious tradition, psychology and other cultural manifestations.

Christian doctrines of the "fall" and "original sin" challenge us to take seriously human responsibility for what we perceive to be evil in the world. If we assume a single human nature throughout life, these doctrines must mean that children too share this responsibility. Freudian psychoanalytic theory posits sexual and aggressive drives which the human being, from earliest childhood, has no choice but to release in one way or another. Some more recent psychological theorists, on the other hand, do not locate aggression in the child by nature, but tend to see the child as good, aggression arising in reaction to adult attitudes and treatment.

Our attitudes about the good and/or evil of children are vitally important. If we believe that there is evil in children, this belief may seem to justify authoritarian forms of relationship with them, punishment for their aggression, and efforts to train them to be good. A belief, drawn from harmful understandings of the fall and original sin, that the female is temptress and the cause of "man's" sin, may seem to justify the sexual exploitation of female children and of women in general. Belief that there is evil in children may serve as a rationalization, in short, for abuse.

The most difficult point to grasp is that any attitude about good and evil in the child is a form of contempt, because it fails to respect the individuality of the child. Whether we see "the child" as good, as evil, or as a combination of good and evil, we fail to accept and relate to a particular, individual child as he or she truly is, whatever that may mean. We need to move beyond all attitudes to unbiased relationship with children.

We cannot know the nature of "the child" in the abstract. We can only live in relationship with a particular child's unfolding being as he or she exists in the world. Rather than relating directly to particular children as they are, however, we take an attitude toward "the child," attribute our attitude to the child's "nature," and then try to relate to all children based on that attitude. In fact, a child's nature can only be "known" in the process of relationship, and thus it can never be known once and for all. Any fixed attitude shields us from true relationship. What we learn about children in true relation ship may be quite different from what we have experienced in the past, in relationships based on attitudes about them.

God's relationship with children indicates that we adults must respect as well as love children. Jesus says that when we receive a child in the name of Christ, we receive Christ, God the Child incarnate, and therefore we must take all children, and our inner child-selves, with ultimate seriousness.

Unfortunately, however, most adults behave more like Adam and Eve than like Mary and Joseph. Adam and Eve, along with the rest of us, fell into sin as a result of an "attitude problem."

God created humankind, male and female, in the image of God (Gen 1:26–27), in a relationship with God and each other of wholeness, harmony and grace. The apparent evil and separation from God in the world have led theologians through the ages to speculate as to the origin of that evil and separation. The book of Genesis relates the story of what Christian theologians have come to call the "original sin" of humankind and the resulting "fall" of humankind from God's grace, as follows:

> Now the serpent was more subtle than any other wild creature that the Lord God had made. He said to the woman, "Did God say, 'You shall not eat of any tree of the garden'?" And the woman said to the serpent, "We may eat of the fruit of the trees of the garden; but God said, 'You shall not eat of the fruit of the tree which is in the midst of the garden, neither shall you touch it, lest you die.' " But the serpent said to the woman, "You will not die. For God knows that when you eat of it your eyes will be opened and you will be like God, knowing good and evil." So when the woman saw that the tree was good for food, and that it was a delight to the eyes, and that the tree was to be desired to make one wise, she took of its fruit and ate; and she also gave some to her husband, and he ate. Then the eyes of both were opened, and they knew that they were naked; and they sewed fig leaves together and made themselves aprons (Gen 3:1–7).

At least two distinct ways of understanding human sinfulness have developed in the history of Christian thought. St. Augustine identified the original sin of Adam and Eve as their love of something other than its proper object, God. He believed that sinfulness was transmitted to all human beings, from generation to generation, by the act of procreation. Sinfulness thus was an inescapable part of human existence at least from the time of birth. Humankind fell from the goodness of creation and thereby distorted the image of God in which we were created, while leaving our human nature intact, according to St. Augustine.[1] In the Augustinian line of thought, some of the Protestant reformers later characterized the fallen sinful state as "total depravity." According to this understanding of human nature, it is necessary to mold and punish the child; nevertheless, there is no real hope of transformation, at least not in this lifetime. It may be possible to punish sin and to restrain the sinner from overt evil, but this restraint does not alter the fallen human state.

A second set of views of the fall and original sin sees human sinfulness as a matter of imperfection that can be corrected. These lines of thought have grown out of the theology of Irenaeus of Lyons and the theology of St. Thomas Aquinas. Irenaeus posited that human ills are the result of incomplete development and that, in the life of the individual and in human history, there can be movement toward greater moral perfection. St. Thomas believed that in the fall human beings lost only special gifts, not essential created goodness, and that human transformation is possible during earthly life (at least in the case of men—Aquinas exhibited an extreme prejudice against women). These lines of theology too invite intervention, although the intention here may be less punitive and more oriented toward seeing that the child develops in the desired way. The developmental view has become increasingly popular among theologians as the harsh Augustinian theology of the fall and original sin has fallen from fashion.[2] The developmental view implies that the greatest imperfection lies at the beginning of life (of humankind and of the individual) and that we can achieve greater perfection as life goes on.

It seems that in our lives the opposite is often true, however. The wholeness of the young child, which if left intact might indeed allow growth and development in God's image, is instead broken due to the forced rejection of the child's child-self. The development of psychically split children does not produce perfection; human perfection can grow only out of the already existing perfection of the image of God in the whole individual, born literally as a new creation.

Even if we should reject an attitude that there is inherent evil in the human child, it would be too simple to eliminate the theology of the fall altogether. If there is no fall, why did contempt for the child ever arise? The depth of human sinfulness may be revealed in the fact that, with the best of intentions, adults cause children to reject their child-selves and thus break their wholeness, whether through adult contempt alone or through more overt forms of child abuse.

There is, however, another way of understanding the Genesis account: God created the world, including human beings, looked at everything created and said that all is very good (Gen 1:31). God reserved the sole right to judge the good and evil of creation—human beings were not to eat of the fruit of the tree of the knowledge concerning good and evil. Adam and Eve, however, concluded that they should open their eyes and see for themselves what is "good" and what is "evil" (Gen 3:1-7). They did not trust God's judgment that creation is good. In attempting to judge the good and evil of elements of creation for themselves, they adopted a fragmented view of creation, no longer seeing it as a whole, no longer seeing the goodness of creation in terms of its wholeness. The story of the tempting serpent may point to their motivation: Adam and Eve saw something (a serpent) in creation that they did not like and they called it "evil." Once they had judged one thing in creation, they judged others—and even themselves—and finally they rejected even the nakedness of their own bodies (Gen 3:7-11). They adopted an attitude toward elements of creation in terms of their good and/or their evil, from a limited human point of view.

Genesis describes the serpent as "subtle," and indeed there is subtlety in the original sin, for Adam and Eve did not merely label parts of creation "evil." The actual original sinful act involved seeing that something (the forbidden fruit) was good (for food). The problem lay in judging what the fruit was "good for." God had already seen that the fruit was good, as part of creation, but its goodness in itself did not mean that it was good for human consumption. The knowledge of good and evil belongs to God alone.

God says "good" of the whole of creation. Human beings say "good" and/or "evil" of elements of creation and as a result attempt to eliminate what they see as evil and mold what they see as good to their own uses. In the case of a human being, use is abuse. This is the fall—a fall from the wholeness of creation into splitness, into broken-ness, as human beings reject or conditionally accept elements of cre-ation. Thus adults in their fallen state pass on sinfulness to children by rejecting certain of their feelings and perceptions, while accepting children on condition that they feel, perceive and behave in ways adults desire. Adults follow the example of Adam and Eve when they fail to accept the whole child as created and use children for their own purposes, finding them "good for" whatever makes the adult feel good. The sinfulness that is passed on is the result of brokenness itself; it is the tendency of brokenness to break wholeness in others.

In the Genesis account, until the fall, "evil" had no meaning except in the context of the commandment not to eat of the fruit of the tree of the knowledge concerning good and evil. God thus defined "evil" in terms of the human potential to usurp the judgment of the good or evil of creation. God defined "good" in terms of what cre-ation is and what God intends for it. The fall comes from the human failure to accept God's creation on God's terms. The commandment is inherent in creation because human creatures can attempt to usurp the judgment of what only the Creator may properly judge—the goodness or evil of creation. Only the Creator can know whether creation is as intended, and therefore good, or is a distortion of the divine creative plan, and therefore evil. If we judge creation, which God has judged good, we judge the judgment of God, placing our-selves above God. We judge God. We become "like gods." We have contempt for God as creator when we have contempt for children or any other part of God's creation. In effect, we say to God, "You bungler! Can't you do anything right? This creation of yours will never amount to anything." We think we can do better. We think we can mold children into acceptable human beings. We think we have the right to judge what they are good for, according to our purposes.

This human judgment—the act, not the capacity to judge—is itself what is evil. We tend to call "evil" whatever injures or causes pain. We thus may see evidence of evil in natural disasters as well as in human acts of violence or self-destruction. We may even call some-thing "evil" simply because we find it unpleasant, frightening, or inconvenient. In fact, however, "evil" is whatever breaks created wholeness and separates us from God. We call "evil" anything in creation that causes us pain, but it is not pain that separates us from God and from ourselves. It is the rejection of pain and other feelings, a rejection resulting from our attempt to judge even those feelings "good" or "evil," that separates us from God and breaks our wholeness.

It seems to me that respecting and preserving the wholeness of children and of all creation requires a sort of mystical detachment. As soon as we prefer one thing, we reject other things. If we want a child to be a certain way, we reject the way the child actually is or might become. When our contempt and the pain and humiliation we inflict make a child wish not to be a child, we make the child reject the way the child actually is, and similarly we reject the way we ourselves actually are. The mystic Meister Eckardt valued detachment even above love. If we adopt an attitude of preferring love to hate, for example, we may reject real feelings of hate and cause splits and repressions, breaking wholeness. Of course we do not desire to feel or to receive hate, and we must not pretend that we do—that would be a rejection of another real feeling, the desire for love. But we can and must accept that hate too is a real, God-given feeling that is part of the creation God has called "good."

An attitude is a movement of the rational intellect. Feelings, unless attitudes obstruct them, arise without regard to rationality, and it is feelings that we must learn to accept and respect. The hate that God gives is a feeling that arises from deep within, under circum-stances of extreme provocation, not a hateful attitude of mind that perpetuates feelings of hate or removes or extends such feelings from their natural context. Acceptance of the feeling of hate as it naturally arises allows an expression of the feeling that is not destructive, so that the feeling can pass and give way to love. The judging intellect must bow to the wholeness of the person. Detachment is the only state of mind that avoids attitudes and does not interfere with the acceptance of feelings. Attachment to attitudes about feelings stands in the way of real engagement on a feeling level.

A Zen poem expresses well the necessity of avoiding such attitudes, or rational judgments:

> The Perfect Way knows no difficulties
> Except that it refuses all preference.
> If you would see the Perfect Way manifest
> Take no thought either for or against it.
> To oppose what you like and what you dislike,
> That is the malady of the mind.
> Do not try to find the truth,
> Merely cease to cherish opinions,
> Tarry not in dualism.
> As soon as you have good and evil
> Confusion follows and the mind is lost.
> When the unique mind is undisturbed
> The ten thousand things cannot offend it.
> When no discrimination is made between this and that
> How can a biassed and prejudiced vision arise?
> Let-go, leave things as they may be.
> If you wish to follow the path of the One Vehicle
> Have no prejudice against the six senses.
> Whereas in the Dharma itself there is no individuation
> The ignorant attach themselves to particular objects.
> The enlightened have no likes or dislikes.
> Gain and loss, right and wrong,
> Away with them once and for all!
> The ultimate end of things, beyond which they cannot go,
> Is not subject to rules and measures.
> Everything is void, lucid, and self-illuminating.
> There is no strain, no effort, no wastage of energy.
> To this region thought never attains.

In not being two all is the same
All that exists is comprehended therein.
It matters not how things are conditioned,
Whether by "being" or by "not being."
That which is is the same as that which is not.
That which is not is the same as that which is.
If only this is realized,
You need not worry about not being perfect![3]

Looking at creation today, it would be difficult indeed not to
conclude that much that we see is a distortion of God's creative plan.
The birth of a child is, however, one place where we can see God's
creation afresh. Every newborn infant is literally a new creation. Able
to see such infants only through eyes accustomed to see creation in a
certain way, however, most human parents through the centuries
have looked at their children in the manner of Adam and Eve and
have said that they are not altogether good in themselves, as they are
created, but are at least in part evil, or are good for what others want
from them.

Becoming like gods, parents mistake themselves for the creator of
their children, thinking that they can improve on creation. They
think their children should be what, as they see it, is good for themselves. They try to replace what God intends with what they intend.
Even when ostensibly acting for their children's own good, parents
pass on the belief learned from their parents that children must be
punished for evil and molded toward the good, in human terms. Thus
they pass on the effects of the fall from one generation to another.
Having been reared in this atmosphere of contempt for the child and
for God, children, when grown, can only rear their children in the
same way.[4] Brokenness produces more brokenness.

By tasting the knowledge concerning good and evil, human beings thus inevitably lose the goodness God gives and produce the evil
they seek to avoid. They presume to know what it would mean to be
true to the image of God, when all they actually can do is discover
what this means by accepting unaltered human nature as found in the
child. The fall is perpetuated not in the failure of the human effort to
improve or to punish, but in the effort itself, in use of the child for

adult purposes, and in the underlying failure to accept God's estimation of creation as good in itself, for God's purposes.

Acceptance of God's estimation does not mean, however, that
we too must pronounce creation in all its aspects (including our children) "good." The meaning of the commandment not to eat of the
tree of the knowledge concerning good and evil is that only God may
judge the evil or the good of creation. We may properly say "good"
only of God (Mk 10:18). Acceptance of God's estimation of the
goodness of creation means acceptance of creation-as-it-is-created-to-
be, of being-as-it-is in each newborn child, a new creation in the
image of God. Goodness in creation is always God's gift, not something that we can judge, produce or enhance. The effort to change or
to improve what God has created can only distort the image of God in
the human child.

"Goodness" in creation means that God did not botch the job.
God created just as God intended to create, and continues to do so in
the new creation of each newborn child. The point is not whether
creation is or is not good according to any standard we might establish. Its goodness is not something we can judge, but only something
we can live out in acceptance of self and others, in mutual respect and
care, in belief in the value of every human being—in other words,
seeing Christ, the image of God, in every human creature, and loving
God, self, and neighbor as self. The God-given goodness of creation
means that we can look at the newborn child and say, "This is being-
as-it-is, which is as it is supposed to be. God says it is good. We can
trust it. We do not have to fear that it will be evil. We do not have to
decide what it will be good for, and we have no right to say that it will
be good for nothing." We may not claim created goodness for ourselves unless we call every other human being good too. Our only
goodness is God-given to us as God's creatures, not as separate individuals but as part of the whole of creation. It does not belong to us
personally or as adults or as members of a particular race, sex, class,
ethnic group, or nationality. God still gives the gift of the goodness of
creation even when we reject the gift by our attitudes toward
creation.

Until we are able to give up our attitudes about good and evil in children, we would do better to accept God's estimation that all of creation is good, including children, than to go on thinking of children as partly evil. Our attitudes and expectations do have an effect. The Bible says, "seek and you will find." It has been my observation that what you seek, you will tend to find, and what you expect to find, you will tend to produce. It seems to me that believing in "a bent toward evil"[5] in children can only produce evil, while believing that children are Christ among us, the new creation in the image of God, can only promote the wholeness of the creation that God has called "good." The expectation for the child that promotes wholeness is the expectation that the child will be what God created him or her to be, not that the child will be good for something in particular, not that life with the child will be free of conflict, and not necessarily that the child will be what you or I might want the child to be.

CHAPTER 5

Feelings and Evil:
Some Religious Views

Rethinking the fall and original sin along the lines suggested in Chapter 4, we find that the Genesis account reveals the theological necessity of avoiding attitudes about good and evil in creation. Besides showing contempt for God, such attitudes in relation to children result in their rejection of parts of themselves, the feelings and perceptions that they associate with being children and that subject them to adult contempt and, in some cases, other forms of abuse. The inner adult-child split then spreads from generation to generation as the individual who has suffered contempt and rejected her or his own child-self cannot avoid having contempt for others who are smaller or weaker, including the children in the next generation. Brokenness begets brokenness.

It seems to me that "evil" is whatever breaks wholeness in creation. Contempt and other forms of abuse, including the belief that there is evil in children, break wholeness in children, forcing them to have contempt for their own childness, to reject and split off their child-selves and all the unbearable feelings that go with experiences of humiliation and abuse. It is this inner adult-child split that leads to abuse in the next generation, and to other forms of oppression in the world as well. Adults who in childhood had to split off their child-selves cannot empathize with the less powerful, but have contempt for them while at the same time fearing them. Thus they can rationalize oppression. The evil of the adult-child split is then lived out and acted out in the many manifestations of brokenness in the world.

The theological understanding of the fall and original sin that I have suggested expresses what is harmful about attitudes concerning good and evil. Some other interpretations of the fall and original sin, however, have themselves contributed to such harmful attitudes, in taking the Genesis account to mean that there is evil in human beings. The belief that there is evil in a fallen and sinful humankind has sometimes amounted to contempt for children and their feelings. Adults, proclaiming the sinfulness of all humankind, often act toward children as if adults were somehow on a higher moral or spiritual plane, as if they had outgrown a "childish" sinfulness and therefore could judge what would make a "good" human being and could re-make children in their image of goodness.

This contemptuous judgment of children and assumption of the right, in effect, to recreate children in a human image of goodness, rather than allowing them to develop according to God's image, have sometimes meant that the doctrines of the fall and original sin have served as rationalizations for abuse. The abused child has every right to feel such feelings as anger, rage, and hate toward the abuser, but the abuser cannot accept the child's reactive aggression. Even if an abusive parent feels helpless and remorseful, to lessen guilt feelings and to stop the child's reactive aggression, the abuser may label the abused child's reactive aggression "evil" and rationalize the abuse: the "bad" child deserves a "good" whipping, must be controlled, must be made to be "good."

A woman who appeared on a television talk show related how her alcoholic mother had abused her when she was a child, swinging her against a radiator while telling her that she had to "beat the devil out of her." When a girl whose parent had beaten her went to parochial school, covered with bruises, and asked for help, a nun told her that she must be a good girl and then her mother would not beat her.

"Wisdom" literature in the Bible unfortunately adds weighty support to this kind of attitude:

> He who spares the rod hates his son,
>   but he who loves him is diligent to discipline him (Prov 13:24).

> Folly is bound up in the heart of a child,
>   but the rod of discipline drives it far from him (Prov 22:15).

Do not withhold discipline from a child;
   if you beat him with a rod, he will not die.
If you beat him with the rod
   you will save his life from Sheol (Prov 23:13–14).

The rod and reproof give wisdom,
   but a child left to himself brings shame to his mother (Prov 29:15).

He who loves his son will whip him often,
   in order that he may rejoice at the way he turns out. . . .
Pamper a child, and he will frighten you;
   play with him, and he will give you grief.
Do not laugh with him, lest you have sorrow with him,
   and in the end you will gnash your teeth.
Give him no authority in his youth,
   and do not ignore his errors.
Bow down his neck in his youth,
   and beat his sides while he is young,
Lest he become stubborn and disobey you,
   and you have sorrow of soul from him.
Discipline your son and take pains with him,
   that you may not be offended by his shamelessness (Sir 30:1–13).

Several contemporary "Christian" child care books that advo-
cate corporal punishment pick up on this kind of thinking. One of
them asserts: "Your child is bent toward evil because he is born
spiritually dead."[1] "No matter how beautiful and well-formed a newborn may be, the Scriptures declare he is, by nature, alienated from
God."[2] "You can love him with all your heart, more than life itself,
but you must face the fact that he is marred and fallen because of
sin."[3] The author states that "[i]t is essentially the father's job to
establish standards,"[4] and he takes this harmful understanding of the
fall to justify physically striking a child:

In the application of the rod, we do not allow the child to refuse
to cry nor to scream in a wild rage. He knows that. When the
child cries, he flushes out his guilt; he clears his conscience. But

when a child screams with rage, he is expressing anger. We don't permit that.

On one occasion we had to spank one of our children four times. The first time for the disobedient act, the next three times for the rage until he cried softly.

You say, "Wow! That's unfair." No. That's biblical. It is also quite effective. It helps curb and break that stubborn asser- tive self-will. As soon as the discipline had ended, there was a submissive spirit. We do not quit until there is. Then love is instantly applied.[5]

When we talk about disciplining and discipling our chil- dren, we're not talking about crushing their spirits. That's cruel and totally unbiblical. We are, however, talking about breaking and curbing his assertive self-will.[6]

It is not uncommon to hear of incidents of abuse in which a parent seems unable to hold back and strikes or otherwise injures a child to make the child's crying or screaming stop. Even recognizing how helpless the parent may feel, or how remorseful once the abusive act is done, we have little difficulty identifying the act as abuse when a parent has lashed out in anger. It may be more difficult, however, to see the abuses in "discipline" meted out in the name of Christian values.

"Christian discipline," calmly and calculatedly administered, may abuse the child both physically, in the use of the rod (or "spank- ing"), and emotionally, in humiliating the child, in breaking the child's will, in forcing submission to the adult's greater power, and in refusing to accept the child's natural reactive feelings (rage, anger), while requiring the expression of other supposedly repentant feelings. Such "discipline" manifests adult contempt for the child and result- ing overt forms of abuse. A slave too will be submissive after physical and emotional abuse and humiliation.

The greatest harm is done in the rejection of a child's natural feelings. Anger is listed among the seven deadly sins, and anger and other aggressive feelings, such as rage and hate, are the feelings we most often label "evil" and reject in the name of Christian values.

According to certain teachings in the Jewish and Christian traditions, the expression of certain feelings, especially hate toward one's
parents, is evidence of a sinful nature, deserving of punishment. The
torah provides, for example, "Whoever curses his father or his mother
shall be put to death" (Ex 21:17). Adults through the ages thus have
branded "evil" whatever is painful or disagreeable to them. St. Augustine condemned the aggression of children, although he seemed to
recognize the child's lack of actual power over adults. He wrote that
an infant's crying and aggressive demands demonstrate "that, if babies are innocent, it is not for lack of will to do harm, but for lack of
strength."[7]

Finding children's hostile feelings threatening, adults react as if
it were the child who had the greater power. Adults overestimate the
child's ability to hurt or control them, and thus rationalize controlling
children with force. The adult's fear of the child's power comes from
the adult's own childhood sense of weakness in relation to powerful
parents. Typically the adult rejected and repressed or split off such
feelings of weakness in childhood, but they have a way of cropping up
again in relation to the adult's own children.[8]

The same repressed sense of weakness that impels adults to reject
the aggressive feelings of children may also lead them to reject children's expressions of weakness, neediness and pain. Adults cannot
accept in the child what they cannot accept in themselves, and the
child's weakness threatens them with awareness of their own childhood experiences of pain, weakness, and humiliation.[9] Accordingly,
adults are likely to deny the seriousness of a child's expressions of
pain. St. Augustine, indeed, saw sin in a baby's crying.[10] It would
seem amazing today to think as St. Augustine did that a baby's crying
is a sign of sinfulness. A tiny infant does not cry willfully or out of
spite but out of need, or in reaction to abuse.

Today in the therapeutic setting, at least, aggressive feelings as
well as expressions of pain usually meet with respect rather than
condemnation. It seems to me that a psychological truth that is necessary for healing in the therapeutic or pastoral setting cannot be at odds
with theological truth. Fortunately, many clergy in pastoral roles have
come to accept and support the individual with all his or her feelings.

In teaching and preaching roles, however, some of the same clergy may resort to harmful doctrine, including the idea that there is sin in the expression of certain feelings, especially aggressive feelings on the part of a child toward an adult.

While psychologically educated people today would not say that any feeling is sinful, many adults (including clergy) are likely to make distinctions between feelings and their expression: the child is not bad, but what the child has done is bad. Having feelings is not the same as verbally expressing those feelings (thus, death for cursing one's parents, according to Exodus), or aggressively acting them out.

It is often insufficient, however, to make nice distinctions between feelings and their expression. The message that often comes through, especially to the person who has suffered abuse, is that the feelings themselves are sinful. Abuse victims will experience as further abuse facile condemnations of hate and admonitions to forgive. And for small children, it is too fine a distinction to differentiate feelings from actions. After all, actions do flow from feelings. If a child is punished for actions that flow from aggressive feelings, the child is likely to conclude that anger is bad and try to do away with anger, usually then acting out the anger unconsciously. Punishment thus will lead to the repression and/or splitting-off of feelings that adults seem to reject, including neediness and pain as well as rage and hate. To preserve an angry child's wholeness, an adult must acknowledge the child's feelings and help the child to find a way of expressing or venting such feelings that will not be harmful to others.

Making distinctions among feelings, their expression, and actions flowing from them too often covers up what actually is a rejection of feelings. We may think that we accept a child's feelings, but being on the receiving end of a child's anger, rage, or hate is another story. We may also feel pushed to the limit by a baby's seemingly unending crying and constant need for attention.

How then can we avoid taking harmful attitudes toward the feelings of children? Is it really possible to go beyond attitudes concerning their good and evil and enter relationship with children without the apparent shelter of such attitudes? The "enlightened" approach to accepting feelings referred to above draws heavily on psychological insights. Some of these insights may help us to move, in accordance with a new theological understanding, beyond attitudes to relationship. Let us look, therefore, at ways that psychology itself has contributed to our attitudes about children and their feelings and to our ability to enter true relationship with children.

CHAPTER 6

Feelings and Evil: Psychological Approaches and a Personal Experience

ABUSE AND PSYCHOANALYTIC THEORY

Many adult attitudes about children and about feelings have grown out of, or in reaction against, the theories of Sigmund Freud. According to Freudian psychoanalytic theory, aggressive feelings are manifestations of one of two innate human drives, the aggressive drive and the sexual drive. According to Freud, these drives (or instincts) inevitably push toward expression, even in young children.

Freud initially believed his patients when through hypnosis he uncovered their repressed childhood memories of sexual abuse by adults (most frequently their fathers). But finally Freud retreated from his earlier findings, because of pressure from the medical establishment of his time, and because he was unable to believe that so many fathers, including perhaps his own, could have been so abusive. Freud wrote:

> Then there was the astonishing thing that in every case blame was laid on perverse acts by the father, my own not excluded.[1]

In defense of the fathers, Freud concluded that an innate sexual desire of the child for the parent of the opposite sex had caused his female patients to fantasize their fathers' alleged sexual acts. To account for the rage that Freud no doubt felt in reaction to his father's "perverse acts," which he did not want to accept as real, he hypothesized innate aggression, expressed in the male child's desire to kill his father, who supposedly stood between the child and his innately desired sexual object, his mother. (Freud never succeeded in reconciling the male and female versions of this theory.) Freud could more easily accept the idea that his father was a hated sexual rival than the apparent reality that his father, like many other fathers, had abused his child and that he hated and desired to kill his father in reaction to the abuse. Freud's drive theory thus solidified the defensive idealization of the father.[2] Rejecting the truth of their experiences, Freud abandoned the inner child-selves of his patients and of himself.

There is a certain similarity between the Freudian and certain religious points of view. Both see the child as the source of undesirable or "bad" feelings and actions, whether because of a fallen, sinful nature or because of an innate human drive. Thus in some sense aggression is the individual child's responsibility according to both views. The religious and psychoanalytic responses arising out of these somewhat similar attitudes do differ, however. Religious tradition calls on human children (and the adults they become) to honor their parents, to recognize their sinfulness and to repent. Freudian psychoanalytic theory calls on them to make conscious their repressed wishes to possess one parent sexually and kill the other, and to sublimate their sexual and aggressive drives.

Some more recent psychological theorists have rejected Freud's drive theory and, at least by implication, the idea that the child is born with a sinful nature. The tendency among theorists such as Guntrip, Kohut, Winnicott, and Miller is to see aggression not as innate but as reactive, brought on initially by the way adults treat children.[3] The various forms of contempt and abuse are among the attitudes and behaviors toward children that, according to this approach, elicit children's rage, anger, hate, and aggressive behavior. Alice Miller asserts that "in the last analysis, our status and degree of power determine whether our actions are judged to be good or bad."[4] She believes that the very treatment designed to make children good, to mold and correct them, produces reactive aggression which children must repress or split off and, later in life, discharge onto others, especially their own children.[5]

There is an increasing willingness, medically, psychotherapeutically, and judicially, to believe children's allegations of abuse and to support adults who are going through the painful process of dealing with childhood abuse or even of discovering the fact that they were abused as children. This willingness implies a rejection of Freud's drive theory. In the context of sexual abuse, the more enlightened approach recognizes that sexual desire for an object belongs to the adult, not the child. When sexual abuse occurs, the adult, abetted by Freud's drive theory, may project that desire onto the child and then use the child's supposed sexual desire as an excuse for the adult's abusive actions.[6] This projective and sexual use of the child expresses contempt for the child's true feelings and needs, as well as for the child's bodily integrity.

A Personal Experience of Aggression

Having been through the agony of unearthing my own childhood experiences of abuse and experiencing my own reactive anger, rage, and hate toward my abuser, I am inclined to agree with theorists who reject Freud's drive theory and believe that the child's nature is just what it should be. I did not desire my father's sexual advances, and I did not fantasize them. Nor did I choose to hate him. As a young child I repressed all recollection of what occurred. It was extremely difficult to believe what I began to remember in adulthood.

Remembering itself is extraordinarily difficult, especially in the face of the abuser's overt or implicit denial, when the context is of one or more events that occurred at a very early age, perhaps in the dark, and outside any normal sequence of events that might be called "real" in the child's ordinary experience. During my childhood my abuser's denial was implicit; he had no need to deny explicitly what I was unable to conceptualize or speak about, at least not in the absence of a great deal of understanding and support, which were not forthcoming. My mother was distant physically and emotionally. At the time of the earliest incidents, I was not yet able to talk. I could only repress the experiences and the feelings that went with them. I had no way of processing or integrating what happened to me.

Several years ago I entered psychotherapy with a psychologist whose education went beyond his essentially Freudian training. Following my psychotherapist's occasional suggestions over a three year period that I had been abused in some way in childhood, based on the evidence of my dreams as well as my difficult relationships with men, I finally was able to become conscious of sketchy memories and their attendant feelings. It would have been so easy at first to push the images and feelings away again, and it was very difficult to resist the urge to do so. Fortunately, I was in a strongly supportive church community and also had the help of a priest whom I could trust thoroughly when the process of remembering began. The memories came as fleeting, fragmentary visual impressions, and much more vividly as patterns of feelings: fear, horror, disgust, dirtiness, humiliation, helplessness, and despair, followed later by anger, rage, hate, and the desire to destroy my father in the most horrible possible way. I could understand at last the sense of revulsion which for many years I had been conscious of feeling toward my father.

My hate and murderous wishes proved a great obstacle to accepting my own childhood reality. It was unthinkable, unspeakable. With a Christian upbringing, how could I think or say that I hated my father, that I wished to kill him (even though I knew that I would not act on this wish)? And yet, those were my feelings. They brought unbearable guilt, and from time to time I could see how all my life I had protected my father and myself from knowledge of my hate. Guilt led to insidious doubt, which ate away my sense of reality about having been sexually abused. My abuser's denial, now explicit, was part of a lifelong family pattern of denials that had impaired my ability to trust my own feelings and perceptions of reality.

My psychotherapist helped me to believe in the possibility that I had been abused and to accept the first memory when it came, but even with the best intentions he repeatedly undermined my very tenuous ability to hold onto a sense of reality about the abuse. When we discussed my dreams, which became more and more clear about the abuse, he spoke of them as "additional evidence." In response, I felt that the reality of the abuse was not established, that it would only be real if I could prove it, which I could not do. In addition, my therapist did not seem totally accepting of my aggressive feelings. He repeatedly reminded me of the undoubted pains and hardships of my abuser's own childhood. He seemed to identify with my father, saying what a pretty little girl I must have been. He suggested that my father loved me and merely expressed his love inappropriately. In addition, the therapist repeatedly told me that I was being seductive toward him. The message I received was that the childhood abuse might be real and might not, but, if it was real, I was at least partly responsible, my abuser was as much a victim as I, and I must forgive and forget.

Gradually, without the unqualified belief and support that I needed from my therapist, and under the double pressure of guilt and gnawing self-doubt, I gave up believing in the reality of what I had learned so painfully. Continuing to press the issue in the face of my father's denials and my therapist's equivocal support so threatened my sense of reality that I could only withdraw, as I had as a child, from feelings and perceptions that seemed to put my sanity at risk. In therapy I let the subject drop. Privately I concluded that I must have imagined the abuse, and I became more and more depressed. It is not difficult to understand Freud's retreat from accepting the reality of abuse, when he had no external support and no doubt was plagued by similar guilt and doubt.

Fortunately, more than a year later, I did find the external support I needed. After reading accounts of other women's childhood experiences of sexual abuse and Alice Miller's book, *Thou Shalt Not Be Aware*,[7] I finally embraced the seemingly unembraceable truth and left therapy. I knew intuitively that the experiences of those other abused women was my experience. I knew their feelings and reactions from the inside. Miller showed me how Freudian theory had helped to enable my abuser (as well as my therapist) to place the blame on me and to deny his own actions. I found that I had to side unequivocally with the only source of reality testing I could find—my child-self, with all her unpleasant and "evil" feelings. The same hate that had been an obstacle to accepting the reality of the abuse became a key to knowing that it was true. Why, after all, would a daughter hate her father so intensely if he had not abused her? All my life I had tried to feel only love toward him. Now my child-self, with the fullness of all my rejected feelings, became my healer. I finally listened only to her voice, as she screamed from deep inside me, "It is true! It really did happen!" She still has to remind me of this truth from time to time.

I did not want my child-self's story to be true, but it has only been in accepting its truth that I have begun to feel whole. I did not want to feel hate. Hate is very painful, one of the most painful feelings I have experienced. I will speak more about the issue of forgiveness in Chapter 12. But, before forgiveness could even become a real issue for me, I had to feel fully all my feelings, including humiliation, helplessness, pain, fear, anger, rage, and hate. I am convinced that my aggressive feelings are reactive, not expressions of an innate drive. I had to feel these previously rejected feelings in full awareness of their childhood origins so that I could be whole and so that I would not displace my aggression and discharge it onto others. I know that as an adult I am responsible for the ways I do or do not choose to express or act on my feelings.

I acknowledge that my personal experience does not prove that all aggressive feelings are reactive in all persons at all times. It seems clear, for example, that genetic and biochemical factors can influence feelings and behavior. But very few adults are violent because of an extra chromosome, and I question how many are violent substance abusers who were not also victims of contempt or abuse as children. Eliminating the aggression that is reactive by stopping all forms of contempt and abuse would, I believe, go a long way to establishing peace on earth.

If we believe in the goodness of God's creation, and if we believe that the new creation is incarnate in each newborn child received in the name of Christ, we must, I think, have faith in the appropriateness of natural human reactions, including aggressive feelings. In ordinary circumstances, when our wholeness has not been broken, we do not hate gratuitously. We hate because of what has been done to us, because of attitudes of contempt and abusive behavior inflicted on us, and our wholeness is broken because we cannot accept and deal with the reality of what has happened to us and the feelings that naturally flow in reaction to what has happened to us. The small child who cannot contain the pain, humiliation, and powerlessness of being treated as a child, or the guilt of feeling such hate, can only submit to the powers of brokenness. Adults' attitudes and behavior often make any other outcome impossible.

AGGRESSION AND RESPONSIBILITY

Hate feels destructive and inwardly disintegrating, but there is an anger that feels strong and healing. This anger is the energy of expansion after we have been shrunk into less, or distorted into other, than our true selves. This anger becomes futile and destructive when we cannot use it to vanquish the contempt and abuse from others that elicit it. Then we hold it in, or turn it against ourselves, and a cycle develops, a cycle of repeated contractions and expansions, that goes on all through life. Each new contraction can give us access to the expansive energy of the old anger. If we do not recognize where the anger originally came from and use its energy inwardly to vanquish self-contempt and self-hate, however, we will continue to displace our old anger and discharge it onto others.

I have said that as an adult I am responsible for the ways I do or do not choose to express or act on my feelings. Current popular psychological wisdom makes a great point of saying that we must take responsibility for our own feelings. We are not to say, "You make me angry," but, "I am angry with you." According to this view, no one can make us feel any feeling; we rather allow them this power over us. I believe that there is a limit to the usefulness of this type of thinking. It implies that we can choose not to have undesired feelings and thus may lead to further repression. We do need to own our feelings, but not necessarily to feel responsible for having them. There are times, in fact, when the feelings of a person, in particular an oppressed person, truly are the responsibility of someone else. It seems appropriate, for example, for a victim of abuse to say to the abuser, "You made me hate you." The abused person does not necessarily want or choose to hate, and the only way of not allowing the abuser this "power" would be to repress or split off the feeling, which would further injure the abused person. Still, the abused person needs to feel the hate as her or his own feeling and to know what aroused it. Then the abused person can feel the feeling and let it go, not allowing it to become entrenched as an attitude. Saying that we take responsibility for our feelings can be a way of protecting those who have injured us or of denying the reality or the significance of what has happened to us. Telling others to take responsibility for their feelings can be a way of denying that we have an impact on others and on their feelings. It makes more sense to me to speak of accepting our feelings than of taking responsibility for them. In fact, those who abuse others are the ones who should take responsibility for the reactive feelings of their victims.

I have pointed out the dangers for abused children of distinguishing among feelings, their expression, and actions arising from them. In terms of adult responsibility, however, I am prepared to make a distinction between feelings and actions. As an adult, I am now in a position of relative power, and I can choose whether, and how, to express the unavoidable hate I feel toward my abuser. Having consciously accepted the feeling of hate and knowing its true object, I can continue to shield my abuser from my hate by avoiding his company. Or, I can say to him, "I hate you." Such an expression of my feelings will not kill him, and it might possibly open up discussion between us, giving him an opportunity to confess his sin, express his remorse, and ask my forgiveness as well as God's. A confrontation of this kind takes a great deal of strength and courage, more that I have thus far been able to muster. Another possibility would be to act on my feelings, to act out the impulse to kill my abuser, or to inflict my rage on someone else smaller and weaker than I. In either case, I would be accountable before God and my neighbor. If I had continued to be unconscious of my hate or its true object, I would have been more likely to act out my hate irresponsibly, inflicting it on others.

Human responsibility may not seem to be as clear-cut an issue as it once did. Often parents who batter their children seem unable to control their actions; indeed, many are living out the consequences of having been abused and having had their wholeness broken in their own childhoods. Are they then responsible for the harm they do? The answer must be yes. The person with the greater power must always be responsible for the use of that power.

If the adult who was abused as a child is responsible for abusive actions toward children, is the child who is being abused then similarly responsible for striking out at an abusive parent? The question of responsibility is different for the child, or for any oppressed person in a position of relative powerlessness in relation to his or her abuser or oppressor. A society's legal system gives an indication of what the society considers evil, or holds its members criminally responsible for. In addition to requiring a measure of sanity and an intent to do harm, we hold individuals culpable only if they have not acted in self-defense. The reactive aggression of the child is in the nature of self-defense. There are even abuse situations in which the abused person is justified in actually killing the abuser in self-defense.

Understanding the rage of the abused child can also help us to understand and trust even the violent protest of oppressed peoples. Just as adults may attempt to justify abuse by pointing to the reactive aggression of abused children, politically dominant groups may attempt to justify discrimination and oppression. When children react aggressively to humiliation and control, adults see their aggression as proof that they need to be controlled. When blacks in South Africa, for example, react with violence to relentless oppression and discrimination—also forms of humiliation and control—whites in power may rationalize their own actual or threatened violence by asserting that black violence proves the need for oppressive control. In 1989 Chinese communist leaders consciously and intentionally used exactly this sort of rationalization in propaganda intended to justify crushing a peaceful movement for democratic reform in China. Protesters acted destructively only in reaction to brutal action by the army, but government television showed the protesters' reactive acts as if those acts had come first and had caused the government to take repressive steps against the people.

Is the violence of such oppressed peoples, or of abused children, then a manifestation of evil? Or is it evidence of a will to resist the evil of oppression, an expression of the will for life and freedom, of created goodness? Thomas Merton wrote understandingly about the impulse to reactive violence in the oppressed:

> "Love" is unfortunately a much misused word. It trips easily off the Christian tongue—so easily that one gets the impression it means others ought to love us for standing on their necks.[8]
>
> Instead of preaching the Cross for others and advising them to suffer patiently the violence which we sweetly impose on them, with the aid of armies and police, we might conceivably recognize the right of the less fortunate to use force, and study more seriously the practice of non-violence and humane methods on our own part when, as it happens, we possess the most stupendous arsenal of power the world has ever known.[9]

In relation to relatively powerless children, adults are the ones with a "stupendous arsenal of power." Adults are the ones who need to recognize the right of the "less fortunate" children to react to oppressive treatment aggressively "and study more seriously the practice of non-violence and humane methods on our own part. . . ." The message of non-violence is a message first and foremost for the powerful. Abusive adults do quite often behave as if abused children "ought to love [them] for standing on their necks." They expect children to honor, respect, and love them, no matter how they treat their children. They insist that children "suffer patiently the violence which [they] sweetly impose on them. . . ." It is only when we more powerful adults accept our own feelings and understand where they come from in our own childhoods that we will be able to stop taking out our pent-up rage and hate in abuse that calls forth more aggression in the next generation.

The nature of children cannot be known except in their relationship with adults, and the nature of adults can only be known in their relationship with children. In some way, we assume that the human adult-child relationship is writ large in the divine Father-Son relationship, and so now let us turn to the inner divine relationship as revealed in the gospel and to our attitudes about "God the Father."

CHAPTER 7

Father and Child:
Image of Relationship

For what man of you, if his son asks him for bread, will give him a
stone? Or if he asks for a fish, will give him a serpent? If you then,
who are evil, know how to give good gifts to your children, how
much more will your Father who is in heaven give good things to
those who ask him (Mt 7:9–11).

As we have seen in the preceding chapters, we adults have a
tendency to adopt attitudes about what we think the nature of the
child is, particularly in terms of the good and/or evil of the child, and
then we try to relate to individual children based on those attitudes.
In fact, however, we can discover a child's nature only in the process
of relationship with that child, and our attitudes shield us from true,
free relationship. These attitudes are a form of contempt, which is the
underlying attitude toward children that makes abuse possible. Thinking that there is evil in a child or in a child's feelings or behavior
enables us to believe that we are justified in punishing the child, often
brutally, and in molding the child to our idea of goodness. If we see
the child's evil in a sexual form, we may feel justified in using the
child sexually. We may see the child as our property, which we feel
free to use as we please. In each case, we see the child as an object, not
as a human being in God's image with whom we are in mutual,
respectful relationship.

We similarly tend to adopt attitudes about God and then try to
relate to God based on our attitudes. Our most striking attitudes about
God, and those that are often most obstructive of true relationship,

attach to our ideas about "God the Father." We think that our attitudes reflect the Father's nature and that what we thus take to be the
Father's nature in turn is a model for us of human fatherhood. If our
experience of human fatherhood has been authoritarian and punitive,
we tend to have the attitude that the Father too is authoritarian and
punitive. We then claim this human idea of divine Fatherhood as a
model for human fatherhood, and often as a rationalization for child
abuse. But the nature of God too can be discovered only in the process
of relationship.

In the incarnation we can glimpse the inner divine relationship
between the first and second persons of the Trinity, Father and
Child. Let us first see what the gospel has to tell us about the Father
as revealed in relationship with the Child incarnate and with us as the
Father's children, and then, in succeeding chapters, we will explore
some of our attitudes about "God the Father" and see how the incarnation responds to them.

The gospel reveals the Father-Child relationship to us as good
news. And this model of relationship is revealed to us in the Father's
relationship to the human child Jesus, the divine Child incarnate.
The relationship of Father and Child is intimate, respectful, and
mutual. The Father attends to the Child's legitimate narcissistic
needs, letting the Child and others know how much "he" values the
Child. The Father's voice says at Jesus' baptism, "You are my beloved
Son; with you I am well pleased" (Mk 1:11b; Lk 3:22b). The Father
knows, and tells others in the Child's presence, that the Child is
worth listening to: "And a cloud overshadowed them, and a voice
came out of the cloud, 'This is my beloved Son; listen to him' " (Mk
9:7). The Child is free to express his feelings to the Father: "And he
said to them, 'My soul is very sorrowful, even to death. . . .' And he
said, 'Abba, Father, all things are possible to thee; remove this cup
from me; yet not what I will, but what thou wilt' " (Mk 14:34–36).
The Child may even express and act on angry feelings, as in the
cleansing of the temple (Mt 21:12ff; Mk 11:15ff; Lk 19:45ff;
Jn 2:13ff).

In the incarnation God also reveals to us a divine-human relationship that is good news. Jesus tells us that it is the Father's good pleasure to give God's reign to us human children, God's "little flock" (Lk 12:32), and that if we ask we will receive (Mt 7:7–8; Lk 11:9–10). The Father accepts us as we are, even if we are tax collectors or sinners, outcast or powerless (Mt 9:10–11). The Father is merciful and provides for our needs even more surely than those of the lilies of the field or the birds of the air (Mt 6:25–34). The Father is more reliable than human fathers in providing for the needs of children (Mt 7:9–11, quoted at the beginning of this chapter).

It is because the Father, who knows us for what we are, loves us that we can dare to look at repressed and split off parts of ourselves and apprehend the good news that the inner adult-child relationship really can be. It is not enough to say that God loves us in spite of who we are. The really good news is that God loves us because of who we are, including our anger, our pain, and our weakness. The incarnation redeems from adult contempt and abuse the child and the inner child-self.

At Gethsemane, after expressing his feelings, saying, "My soul is very sorrowful, even unto death," Jesus addressed the Father as Abba, "Dada" (Mk 14:36). Jesus spoke Aramaic, and Abba is the original word in the Aramaic that Jesus used in all his prayers to address the first person of the Trinity.[1] Translators have usually rendered this form of address as "Father," but their more formal translation misses the significance of the fact that Jesus used an infant's "babbling" sound, a "childish cry."[2] The Father is "intimately close," and the Son incarnate relates to the Father as a child, an infant.[3]

According to St. Paul, the Spirit of the Son in us also cries "Abba" (Rom 8:15; Gal 4:6). To call on God as "Dada," as Jesus did, is to find both the young child in ourselves and the true loving Parent in God who is always there for us because, having directly experienced human childhood in the incarnation of God the Child, God can empathize with us and know and accept us as we are. In God's inner Father-Child relationship as outwardly manifest in the incarnation, God reveals the willingness to enter into God's own Child-self and to take that Child-self seriously. Abba is the Father aspect of a God who dares to experience what it is to be a Son, a divine and human child, and who thus can empathize with inner and outer human children.

Herein lies the implication of the foregoing exploration for the divine model of fatherhood: do as God has done, enter into your own child-self; feel fully what the child feels. Experience the rejection, betrayal, abandonment, humiliation, and abuse that you were not able to feel or express as a child. Feel fully what the child feels, and then you will be able to care for, respect, and learn from your child. To the extent that the experience of childhood is alive within, the adult is alive and able to empathize with children.

God did not become incarnate in order to teach us a lesson, to mold us or punish us, or to show us who is boss, but to be in direct relationship with us. God's experience of God's own Childhood and of human childhood is a real experience of relationship, for God and for us. When God enters the human condition, walks again with us in the garden, the divine-human relationship is direct, revelatory and transforming.

The inner divine relationship is a relationship of whole with whole, wholeness in the Father with wholeness in the Son. The Son, the Child, constitutes an aspect of the wholeness of the Father, and the Father constitutes an aspect of the wholeness of the Child: "He who has seen me has seen the Father. . . . Believe me that I am in the Father and the Father in me" (Jn 14:9–11).

Even in our broken state we reflect the image of God, Father and Son, in which we are created. In human terms, every father is also a son, and every son is also a father. In seeing the father, we see the son he once was, because he contains the child-self within. In seeing the son, we also see the father, because of the son's identification with, and internalization or introjection of, his own father in childhood. "Only a child's unconscious can copy a parent so exactly that every characteristic of the parent can later be found in the child."[4]

We too often think that "God" means "Father." God is triune, but the Sonship of God is hidden from our view in the absence of a true apprehension of the incarnation because of the human blindness to the son in fathers and the father in sons. Adults are too often blinded by the belief that the father is all in importance, the child nothing. The divine Child always remains the Child; the first and second persons of the Trinity are not merged. We too easily lose sight of the good news of God the Child and turn the Son into another image of fatherhood in accordance with our human experiences of fatherhood.

In Jesus, God identifies Godself with the child, born as an infant into this world and ultimately suffering its abuses. Thus God is identified with both sides of the parent-child relationship, and wholeness in that relationship is the image of God. God relates to Godself inwardly as Father, Son and unifying Holy Spirit. The image of God in us is the image of wholeness in relationship, in our relationships inwardly to ourselves and outwardly to each other, and in God's relationship to us. We are created in God's image, and each of us too has an internal relationship of adult-self and child-self, which need not be split but can find unity in the wholeness of the Holy Spirit.

St. Paul tells us that if we have faith we become adopted children of God. As children of broken human parents we internalize and carry the adult-child split as part of our psychic make-up. If we accept God as Parent by faith, we may then internalize and carry God, Parent and Child, not split, but in relationship in the unity of the Holy Spirit, as the unifying basis of our whole being.

CHAPTER 8

"God the Father":
Image of Human Attitudes

Unfortunately we do not always live in true relationship with God, ourselves and each other, in accordance with the divine Father-Child relationship revealed to us in the gospel. We thus fail to be true to the image of God in which we are created. How we look at God and how we look at ourselves are interrelated, interdependent, as are our attitudes toward ourselves as adults and our attitudes toward children. We have made for ourselves other images of "God the Father," often unconsciously, as we project our experiences of human fatherhood onto the "Father" (or onto "God," thinking that the two are identical and thus ignoring the fact that the Father is but one of three persons of the Trinity, all three of whom together comprise God). We then often take the father image we have projected as a divine model for the relationship of adult human beings, especially fathers, to human children.

"GOD THE FATHER": A SEXIST PROJECTION?

Before looking at the attitudes we project onto the "Father," it is necessary to deal with the fact that we are talking about "Father" and not "Mother" or other possible symbols for God. It is true that the Bible uses maternal and other images, some of them not human, such as rock, water, and eagle, to speak about God. But "Father" is the symbol that dominates Christian belief and worship. It is also the symbol most relevant to the adult-child split and to issues concerning child abuse. Most simply, the masculine image dominates because men have been the principal authors of scripture and theology. The projections of human experiences of fatherhood that we mistake for the nature of the first person of the Trinity are male projections. The patriarchal bias of much of our tradition is related to our earthly experience of male dominance, and the first experience that most human beings have of that dominance is in relation to the human father in the family.

According to the masculine ideal, for God to be God, God must be all-powerful, and the most powerful element of early human experience is the father. The earliest impressions are the strongest, and so, seeing ourselves as children in relation to God, we, all having been trained from birth to participate in the masculine view of reality, respond most strongly to the "Father" image. "Father" is the most powerful image because traditionally the father has been the family disciplinarian, an authoritarian figure who requires the respect of women and children, who are considered weaker. This "respect" is quite often actually fear, especially in homes where abuse occurs. A majority of child abuse (and also the abuse of women) is perpetrated by men.

Jesus himself called the first person of the Trinity "Father," or "Dada." But why did Jesus do this? I will explore a possible answer to this question more fully in Chapter 10. Here I will only suggest that the incarnation responds to our human situation. Jesus related to the first person of the Trinity as "Father" because it is precisely human fatherhood that we most need to understand in a new way. It is most often authoritarian fathers playing god who perpetuate the cycle of abuse. Because it is not primarily in a model of motherhood that the cause for our brokenness lies, motherhood is not the key to the healing made possible by the incarnation. Jesus did not have to relate to the first person of the Trinity as "Mother" in order to reveal a trans-formed model of motherhood. Perhaps that is why Jesus, the one who was not subject to human brokenness and sin, had a human mother but not a human father. It is distorted fatherhood that has given us a distorted masculine image of God.

Properly understood, the Father image of the gospel responds to our human condition in a healing and transforming way. The gospel demonstrates the transformation that we need by replacing the model of the father who uses his power to dominate others with the divine model of a Father who serves the needs of those who are less power- ful. The Father revealed in relationship with the Child shows that the authoritarian, punitive "Father" model is an idol, a projection of our experiences of human fathers with their inner adult-child splits.

It will not do any good to dispense with "Father" as a sexist projection unless we let the gospel heal us of the adult-child split and all splits based on the authoritarian model. The feminist critique has begun to free us from an exclusively male representation of God. Seeing things from the child's point of view reveals, however, that adding female images for God does not solve everything. Girls as well as boys are affected by contempt and abuse and are forced to reject their child-selves. In fact, female children receive an extra dose of contempt because they are female. While a boy typically grows up and seems to escape completely the humiliating status of a weaker being, girls grow up to be women who (at least until very recently, and even now in many cases) continue to bear the stigma of weakness. Thus mothers have not generally shared the masculine authoritarian image. Feeling the humiliation of being female in their daily lives, often women have been forced to stay in touch with childhood feelings that they would have preferred to repress, and so they have been able to have greater empathy with children than many men. The more power women gain, and the more successfully they shed the idea of inherent weakness, the greater the danger will be that they will perfect the inner adult-child split and, like many men, will use their power against children. Even now mothers may be as likely as fathers to slap and to humiliate their children. A feminist equality of women and men does not in itself alter the power-based relationship of adult to child. In considering the problem of child abuse, my use of the term "father" therefore refers to any adult who might lack empathy for children and exercise power over them. Of course, I do not mean to suggest that all fathers lack empathy for children or are abusive to- ward children.

AN AUTHORITARIAN MODEL OF "GOD THE FATHER"

Alongside the gospel image of Fatherhood described in Chapter 7, Christian traditions have included other understandings of "God the Father." One harmful image of "God the Father" reflects the projection of our experiences of human fathers whose wholeness has been broken by the rejection of their child-selves. This is a model of fatherhood in which fathers cannot have empathy or respect for children, but have contempt for them and mold, punish, and use them. The adult-child split of these human fathers results in a projected "Father" image that loses sight of God's tri-unity and the inner divine Father-Child relationship, as well as the divine-to-human Father-child relationship, both of which the gospel reveals. We cannot know the Father apart from the relationship of Father and Son, but we try to separate Father from Son/Child, assuming that "Father" alone is "God."

Some fathers take the split image of the "Father," which results from the projection of the experience of broken human fathers, as a divine model for human adult-child relationship. This model reflects the human attitude that, due to the fall and original sin, human beings are at least in part evil. According to this view original sin consists of human disobedience. This image is of a "Father" who judges the good and evil of human beings and is wrathful in reaction to human disobedience and sinfulness. Human fathers are similarly wrathful in reaction to their children's willfulness and disobedience, which such fathers believe are inherent in children due to their fallen human state. Even if the human father consciously thinks that he himself "acts not in anger," he may act out this paternal wrath, however unemotionally, in such forms as humiliation, physical punishment, and the disallowance of the child's feelings (especially anger).

Human beings deem the wrath of the "Father" and of human fathers justified by the nature or the behavior of human beings and of children, and the expression of this wrath is "for their own good," a necessary expression of paternal "love."[1] We define the Father as good and loving, and so "his" wrath must be justified. The wrath of the "Father" teaches sinful human beings that they deserve punish-ment and need salvation. The wrath of human fathers breaks the evil self-will of children and, like the wrath of the "Father," enforces obedience. Believing that one's own father, like "God the Father," is good and loving, but also knowing him to be wrathful, necessitates believing that as a child one is evil, deserving of wrath. We grow up saying, "My father beat me, but I deserved it. It was good for me." The child, when grown up and a parent, then assumes the "Father's" place in the misunderstood "Father"-child relationship, feels himself or herself to be good and loving and, when enraged at his or her children, feels similarly entitled to believe that those children deserve wrath, that punishment is an expression of parental love.

According to the authoritarian model, the "Father," once im-manent in creation, walking in the garden with a humankind created in "his" image, has withdrawn into invisible transcendence, a lofty height from which "he" rewards obedience and imposes the conse-quences of "his" wrath in human history. By their disobedience, human beings have distorted the image of God in which they were originally created. According to this model, the "Father" is separate and different from humankind, and fathers are separate and different from children. The divine-human relationship is split, and the human adult-child relationship is split.

Certain "Christian" discipline acts out the kinds of con-temptuous attitude and abusive treatment that flow from this sort of thinking (conscious or unconscious) about "God the Father." Two nineteenth-century child-rearing guides illustrate such attitudes:

> Even truly Christian pedagogy, which takes a person as he is, not as he should be, cannot in principle renounce every form of cor-poral chastisement, for it is exactly the proper punishment for certain kinds of delinquency: it humiliates and upsets the child, affirms the necessity of bowing to a higher order and at the same time reveals paternal love in all its vigor.[2]

> True love flows from the heart of God, the source and image of all fatherhood (Ephesians 3:15). . . . This hallowed love can

thus be severe even as it can be mild, can deny even as it can bestow, each according to its time; it also knows how to bring good by causing hurt, it can impose harsh renunciation. . . . "Thou shalt beat him (the child) with the rod, and shalt deliver his soul from hell" (Proverbs 23:14).[3]

Just as we must act with humble faith in the higher wisdom and unfathomable love of God, so the child should let his actions be guided by faith in the wisdom of his parents and teachers and should regard this as schooling in obedience toward the Heavenly Father. . . . In the family it is usually weak mothers who follow the philanthropic principle, whereas the father demands unconditional obedience without wasting words. In return, it is the mother who is most often tyrannized by her offspring and the father who enjoys their respect; for this reason he is the head of the whole household and determines its atmosphere.[4]

In his *Confessions,* St. Augustine told of the beatings he received at school and of his parents' contempt for his suffering. Although Augustine had remarkable insight in being able to see the inefficacy as well as the brutality of such treatment, he believed God visited this suffering on him through his parents and teachers for his own good. In fact, he saw the needless childhood suffering as part of his lot as a fallen human being, one of "the sons of Adam":

So I was sent to school to learn to read. I was too small to understand what purpose it might serve and yet, if I was idle at my studies, I was beaten for it, because beating was favoured by tradition. Countless boys long since forgotten had built up this stony path for us to tread and we were made to pass along it, adding to the toil and sorrow of the sons of Adam.[5]

I was still a boy when I first began to pray to you, my Help and Refuge. I used to prattle away to you, and though I was small, my devotion was great when I begged you not to let me be beaten at school. Sometimes, for my own good, you did not grant my prayer, and then my elders and even my parents, who certainly

wished me no harm, would laugh at the beating I got—and in
those days beatings were my one great bugbear.

O Lord, throughout the world men beseech you to preserve
them from the rack and the hook and various similar tortures
which terrify them. Some people are merely callous, but if a man
clings to you with great devotion, how can his piety inspire him
to find it in his heart to make light of these tortures, when he
loves those who dread them so fearfully? And yet this was how
our parents scoffed at the torments which we boys suffered at the
hands of our masters. For we feared the whip just as much as
others fear the rack, and we, no less than they, begged you to
preserve us from it.[6]

In his "Lectures on Galatians" of 1535, Martin Luther ex-
panded on Paul's analogy of the custodianship of the law. In the
course of theological exposition, Luther revealed the harshness of his
own upbringing, in turn shedding light on his theology of the wrath
of God. Luther believed that God crushes us with the law as a necessary preparation for hearing the truth of the gospel. "For God cannot
deny His own nature. That is, He cannot avoid hating sin and sinners. . . ."[7] "Thus a Christian . . . feels that there is sin in him and
that on this account he is worthy of wrath, the judgment of God, and
eternal death."[8] Luther saw humankind as sinful by nature, depraved
in intellect, and having a will hostile to God's will.[9] He explicitly
connected the idea of human, as well as divine, fatherly love with
punitiveness and contempt:

For it is legitimate for an apostle, a pastor, or a preacher to reprove
those under him sharply in Christian zeal; and such scolding is
both fatherly and holy. Thus parents, in fatherly or motherly
feeling, will call their son a foolish or worthless fellow, or their
daughter a slattern—something they would not stand for if someone else did it. . . .

Therefore denunciation and anger are as necessary in every
kind of life as any other virtue is. Nevertheless, this anger must be
moderated and must not proceed from envy; it must proceed only
from fatherly concern and Christian zeal. That is, it must not be a

childish or womanly show of temper that is out for revenge; its only desire should be to correct the fault, as a father disciplines his son, not to set his own mind at rest with a desire for revenge but to improve the son by such discipline.[10]

Thus it happens that the same denunciation can be the greatest benefit if it comes from the mouth of a father, but the worst sort of injury if it comes from the mouth of a peer or an enemy.[11]

But the father's attitude is upright and sincere. If he did not love his son, he would not punish him; he would send him away, despair of his being saved, and let him perish. When he punishes him, this is a sign of his fatherly feeling for his son and is for the son's own good.[12]

The attitude reflected in these portrayals of fatherly "love" is contempt for those who are weak in relation to one who is powerful and wrathful. The "Father" is good. The "Father" is angry. Therefore human beings must be evil. This attitude sees the relationship of a "Father," who is good, powerful, and angry, to human beings, who are evil and relatively powerless, reflected in the relationship of human fathers to human children. Children must obey their fathers, just as human beings must obey the Father. Children are certainly evil; otherwise their loving, good fathers would not punish them. (I illustrate these theological views with quotations from St. Augustine and Martin Luther because they are the rare theologians who disclose personal experiences of childhood abuse. These quotations do not, of course, represent the whole of their theologies, and in neither case do I suggest that the full theological exposition is identical with the authoritarian "Father" model I posit in this chapter.)

Jesus, the Child of God, certainly was obedient to the Father, even to the point of death. If the divine Father-Child relationship of the gospel is a model for human adult-child relationships, must not children be required to obey?

The parent whose inner adult-child relationship is not split will be able to have the true best interests of the child at heart and will not demand obedience as a mere exercise of power over the child. Such a parent will know when to require obedience, for example when it is a matter of the child's health or safety, and the child will be able to appreciate the reason for the requirement. The parent will not limit the child's freedom just "to show who is the boss." (On the subject of appropriate limit setting, see chapter 13.)

Nevertheless, because of the element of power and submission to control in any human requirement of obedience, the Father/father analogy does break down in the context of obedience. The only obedience that does not make us feel limited in our freedom is obedience to God, which in fact makes us feel free. The feeling of freedom is secure only when we are objectively free to be the creatures God created us to be and free to exist authentically out of that being. For the only true human freedom lies within creaturely limits, in a relation of obedience to God. God's power to which we yield is not power over us, but the power in us to be and to exist freely, authentically, as God's creatures. Thus God-given human freedom is not the cause of evil; non-acceptance of the goodness of human beings as created impairs our freedom and causes evil. Freedom and goodness are inseparably God-given. True human freedom is freedom in the Spirit, the wind blowing where it will.

Only the Creator can know in all situations what really is best for each of us individually and in relation to the whole of creation. No one should have to submit to requirements that are at odds with the good of all of us. Parents who are obedient to the will of God by living authentically out of wholeness will not poison their children with contempt and power-based relationships that split their wholeness.

It is true that human brokenness perpetuates itself in the world in a way that manifests what we may call human evil or sinfulness. And it does make sense to suppose that God, whom we assume to be good, would be angry to see the effects of human brokenness being passed along from generation to generation in such forms as the adult-child split and child abuse. Therefore, in light of our explorations of the fall, original sin, and the Fatherhood of God, it is necessary to take another look at the anger of God.

CHAPTER 9

The Wrath of God

According to the model of fatherhood outlined in Chapter 8, the wrath of God is the wrath of the "Father," which is analogous to the anger of human fathers toward their disobedient children. In the Hebrew scriptures we are familiar with the idea of a wrathful "Yahweh," who punishes Israel for idolatry and for inhumane relations with others, such as widows and strangers. It is not clear in "Yahweh's" wrath, however, that it is God as "Father" who is angry. "Father" is a term of address for the first person of the Trinity, a term that rarely appears in our Bible outside the New Testament (although it does also appear in some later Jewish writings that are not included in the Christian Bible[1]). The Hebrew understanding of God is not, of course, trinitarian; while Israel sometimes experienced "Yahweh" as paternal, that is only one of the many ways that Israel experienced the one God "Yahweh." But as we appropriate Hebrew scriptures and interpret them in light of the Christian gospel, we tend to read the image of "Father," which we have come to understand as one of three divine persons comprising one God, back into "Yahweh." Often our understanding of the "Father" is colored by human experiences of fatherhood. We thus merge our human father projections with certain aspects of "Yahweh" and come up with an image of a divine "Father" who is angry and punitive.

We think that God's anger toward sinful human beings is the anger of an adult, a father, toward children. But what about the anger of children who are subjected to adult contempt and often much more flagrant abuses? The child, who enters the world whole, a new creation in the image of God, feels anger in reaction to narcissistic,

emotional, physical, and other wounds inflicted out of adult contempt for the relatively powerless child. Adult anger at children,
which the adult may deem justified by the supposed evil or the bad
behavior of the child, is often anger displaced from the adult's own
childhood, when the adult's own relative powerlessness made it impossible to express or sometimes even to feel the anger.[2] In the context
of abuse and contempt, anger thus properly belongs to the child,
whether the unconscious inner child-self of the contemptuous or
abusive adult or the abused child.

It seems reasonable to me to suppose that actions that produce
the reaction of anger in the child and distort creation by breaking the
child's wholeness also anger God. The feelings of the child, including
reactive anger and hatred, are part of God's creative plan. The child's
reactive anger is an expression of God's anger, a signal from God that
human creation in the image of God is under attack. The wrath of the
child is the wrath of God in reaction to the perversion of creation and
of relationships among creatures, as manifest in oppressive child-rearing practices. Sin against the child is sin against God, because it is
part of the perpetually renewed original sin, ever anew breaking the
interrelated harmony of God's creation, a harmony that can be based
only on mutuality and respect among all creatures. If the child is
rightfully enraged at abuse, why should God not be enraged at the
abuse of creation? God entrusted Godself to human adults as a human
child in the incarnation, and in some sense God continues to entrust
Godself to us in every human child created in the image of God. As
the underlying structure of being of creation, God is personally injured by both the abuse the child receives and by the child's resulting
rejection of her or his child-self, which breaks the child's wholeness
and distorts the image of God in which the child is created.

Church historian and theologian Richard Norris analyzes human
sinfulness as follows:

> [T]he disposition to sin . . . shows itself in a compulsion to domi-
> nate . . . to make sure that other people serve one's own purposes
> and conform to one's own rules. . . . [A]nd this in its turn grows
> out of the anxiety and fear which are generated by the claims of

the "other" to have a place, an inner integrity, and an initiative of its own.[3]

Children have reactive aggressive feelings when adults violate their "inner integrity," acting out "a compulsion to dominate . . . to make sure that [children] serve [adults'] own purposes and conform to [adults'] own rules." Adults fail to perceive that the child, the "other," has a right to "a place, an inner integrity, and an initiative of its own." While, of course, children cannot always have their own way, they must learn the meaning of having a choice by having their choices respected, even when circumstances do not permit us to follow their choices. And at those times, adults must also respect children's reactive feelings. Children's reactive aggressive feelings are messages from God about what is happening in creation. But children must be able to experience and express those feelings in the original childhood context, when they are natural reactions, or aggression becomes split-off and demonic and is ultimately discharged against the self or others.[4]

Accordingly, it is not the father's anger at the child that is analogous to the anger of God. God's anger is the anger of threatened wholeness. God's anger is manifest in the context of the relative powerlessness of the child before any split and is directed at actions that break the child's wholeness and distort the image of God in the child. If the child could fully feel and express all reactive feelings, including anger in reaction to unavoidable frustrations as well as to wrongly exercised adult power, the child could remain whole in God's image and would not have to split off or repress the aggressive or the weak and needy parts of the self. What begins as unavoidable frustration ends as abuse if the child is not free to feel and express all reactive feelings. The child can only experience and express reactive anger, rage, and hate with the help of at least one empathic adult.[5]

Children, with all their feelings and needs, come into the world as God's good creation, and children have the absolute right to be the center of their parents' universe, to have their God-given feelings respected and their God-given needs satisfied. In this limited sense, the child has the right to the adults' obedience rather than the other way around.[6] The right of the child to parental obedience diminishes in proportion to the child's own growing power as the child matures and becomes more capable of mutual relationship.[7]

To many parents, however, it is heresy to see God in their children's feelings and needs. Parents have projected the thwarted God-rights of their own infancy onto "God" and have assumed God-power in relation to their child. Their assumption of God-power never corrects the original failure to have their own God-rights and needs respected and satisfied in childhood. Hitler tried to resume the God-stature of infancy, but this can never be legitimate in adulthood, when actual power is available. The baby may be God in rights and needs because the baby cannot be God in power. The infant is weak, helpless, totally needful. No adult, no person in a position of relative power, has the right to assume God-power in relation to another human being, whether a child or any other less powerful person.

What then happens to the model of divine Father for human fathers? Many adults misunderstand God's anger as being like fathers' anger at their children and then believe that God's anger is a model for human parents. Having projected their misunderstood and displaced anger onto "God," many parents, often unconsciously, claim what they have projected as justification for behaving like wrathful gods toward their children. However, the foregoing exploration of a theology of the fall and the wrath of God coincides with the scriptural revelation that God is not only Father; God is also Child! In God's wrath, God identifies not with the powerful fathers but with the powerless children. As the other liberation theologies assert, God is the God of the powerless. God is on the side of the oppressed. The wrathful "Father" model is an idol. The divine model of fatherhood can come only from the inner relationship of God the Father with God the Child, as we have seen in Chapter 7. "Not that anyone has seen the Father except the one who is from God; he has seen the Father" (Jn 6:46).

The doctrine of the Trinity tells us that the Child aspect of God, the Son, was not created, but is eternally begotten of the Father. In terms of our projections, we might say that, apart from the incarnation, the Child aspect of God is unconscious, just as the inner child-self of the adult whose wholeness was broken in childhood is unconscious. We thus unconsciously project onto "God" a combination of our own God-right from infancy, denied its rightful reign, and the power of adults who played god toward us. In other words, "God" receives the projections not only of the fathers' conscious adult-selves, but also of their split-off and unconscious child-selves. The child-self element is doubly unconscious, unconscious in the fathers themselves, and unconscious in our perceptions of the projected image. The unconsciously projected child-self element contributes to the power that this image of "God" has over us because of the legitimacy of childhood needs that were not satisfied.

When the human split is healed and the adult's child-self becomes conscious, when the adult consciously experiences powerlessness and restores anger to its appropriate context, then the adult can have empathy for children and can truly apprehend the gospel of God the Child. Then children need no longer split off or repress pain or anger, and healed human beings need no longer see in "God" a wrathful "Father."

CHAPTER 10

Projection and the Symbol "God the Father"

As we have seen, much that we often understand "God the Father" to be reflects projections of the human experience of human fathers. These projections, although usually unconscious, form our attitudes about the "Father," attitudes that often stand in the way of direct relationship with the Father as revealed in the gospel. Human projections of fatherhood are particularly obstructive of true relationship and a true apprehension of God when they reflect the adult-child split. These are the projections of fathers who are unconscious of their inner child-selves, having rejected in childhood all the painful and difficult feelings and perceptions that constituted their reality at that time. In rejecting their childhood experiences of contempt, humiliation, pain, need, powerlessness, being used and abused, and reactive anger, rage and hate, such fathers early in life rejected their identity as children, with all the child's weakness and neediness. Such fathers cannot have empathy for their child-selves or for children. Those who experience and project their brand of fatherhood thus see in the "Father" an authoritarian figure who punishes and molds human beings, having no real empathy for human childlike qualities of weakness and need or for a child's natural anger at being abused. The Father of the gospel, in contrast, gives care and respect in relationship with the Child incarnate and with human beings.

Given all the problems that the symbol "Father" seems to raise, we may well wonder why Jesus used that symbol in relating to the first person of the Trinity. Why use a symbol that is loaded for us with all our human experiences of fatherhood? Why use a symbol that seems to exclude female reality from divine reality? In this chapter I am going to explore the possibility that Jesus used the name "Father" precisely because of the human problems of fathers and children. Jesus, the one human being true to the image of God and not subject to the adult-child split, could see our projections for what they are and respond to our predicament with a new model of fatherhood, based on wholeness within the divine inner relationship, which is expressed in the incarnation as the relationship of Father and Son. The use of "Father" in the gospel is not meant to give divine approval to power-based adult-child relationships, to fathers playing god, or to adult contempt for the child, nor does it define God or imply divine masculinity. Rather the "Father" symbol of the gospel responds to and transforms broken human fatherhood, the prototype of all power-based relationships and therefore the aspect of human existence that most needs healing because it is most obstructive of true relationship among human beings and between God and humankind.

I am writing from the point of view of belief in God, and I believe that something of the truth about God is revealed even as we project our human experience onto symbols such as "God," "Yahweh," and "Father." This chapter will be rather abstract (my apologies to LJ), as I attempt to bridge the gap between the "Father" of human projections and what the gospel reveals of the inner reality of God and of God's relationship to us. The abstract discussion of symbolism does, I believe, unearth some important truths for the theology of the Child.

I find some of the theories of Paul Ricoeur helpful as a starting place for exploring possible ways to bridge the gap between our projections onto symbols such as "God" and the self-revelation of God through those same symbols. For Ricoeur, the word is symbol,[1] and the symbolic word is one that has a first meaning which, once addressed, reveals a second meaning:

> Symbols occur when language produces signs of composite degree in which the meaning, not satisfied with designating some one thing, designates another meaning attainable only in and through the first intentionality.[2]

> Hence one and the same fantasy can carry two opposed vectors: a regressive vector which subjects the fantasy to the past, and a progressive vector which makes it an indicator of meaning.[3]

Ricoeur subjects the symbol "God the Father" to regressive analysis by reviewing Freud's understanding of that symbol. According to Freud's Oedipal theory, a central element of human psychic reality centers on the "Oedipus complex," which, Freud says, consists of the young child's sexual desire for the parent of the opposite sex and the attendant desire to kill and replace the same-sex parent. These two desires are necessary expressions of what Freud sees as two innate human instincts, or drives. In other words, according to Freud's view, both sexual and aggressive impulses are present and must be dealt with in some manner, from earliest childhood all through life, regardless of the individual's life experience. Freud says that the Oedipal drama replays in the individual the common human heritage of the actual murder of the original father by his sons in the primal horde. Freud reduces the symbol "God the Father" to human projections of the murdered father of the primal horde, combined with the Oedipal father of the individual, and dismisses as secondary elaboration, similar to the deceptive work of a dream, any further attempt to develop or explain the "Father" image.[4]

Ricoeur accepts Freud's reduction, saying that faith needs the psychoanalysis of religion to remove the idolatrous dimension of the symbol that results from our projections.[5] Unlike Freud, however, Ricoeur finds more in the symbol than our projections. Ricoeur believes that the removal of idolatrous projections can restore the symbol as the horizon through which the sacred (or "Wholly Other") draws near.[6] This is Ricoeur's "progressive vector," which makes the symbol "an indicator of meaning."[7] Ricoeur agrees with Freud that we create the symbol of the sacred out of an infantile desire for consolation and fear of punishment, but, unlike Freud, Ricoeur maintains that the object (God) is real and really does address us and draw near through the symbol. The sacred gives the symbol its reality as symbol, its transparency to the second (or multiple) meaning beyond the opacity of the word. We need to expect to be addressed by the object and to listen and be open to the drawing near of the sacred through the symbol.[8] Having gone backward to the symbol's origins (as Freud sees them), Ricoeur then finds that culture has corrected the original myth, working the symbol forward, by love, toward meaning.[9]

Alice Miller too reduces the symbol "God the Father," but rejects Freud's idea of the primal and Oedipal contents of human projections in favor of an image of a godlike pedagogical father whose feelings of weakness and neediness and whose anger toward his parents from his own childhood are split off and/or repressed.[10] The projection serves to maintain the idealization of the father of childhood in the face of evidence (such as the child's own feelings) of the father's pedagogical cruelty. Ricoeur's view that culture works the symbol forward toward meaning notwithstanding, actual human fatherhood has too often remained at the level of the pedagogical origins of that symbol, according to Miller's review of the use made of the father model in the history of childrearing.[11] By "pedagogy" Miller means the contemptuous attitude and abusive behavior of adults toward children designed to mold them into "good" human beings. Pedagogy may be authoritarian or even anti-authoritarian.[12]

Although, due to contempt and the adult-child split, human projections too often mask the meaning of the symbol beyond those projections, I suggest that not only symbol creation, but also the phenomenon of projection itself, can be understood in the context of God's self-revelation to us. Projection is a normal part of human functioning[13] and thus part of the creation that God pronounced good. The human being in God's image is a medium of the revelation of God. One means or process of this revelation is human symbol creation, and projection is an essential part of symbol creation. God is in both symbol creation and projection and thus is revealed in the process as well as in and through the content of the perceived symbol. Before exploring how projection might work positively in the relationship between God and a fallen humankind, I shall first explore how projection might function if humankind were not fallen.

God's original self-revelation to us is in creation, especially in humankind created in the image of God. When we are true to our creation in the image of God and see ourselves clearly, God is re-vealed. God gives us projection so that we can know a God, not who is "Wholly Other," but who is revealed in the human condition, in ourselves and each other, in all of us as community of God. Apart from the fall, God walks with humankind in the garden (Gen 3:8), and God is visible in creation (Rom 1:20).

Thus, if we were as originally created, we would be able to see God at least partly in God's image, in ourselves. In other words, I suggest that the human being, as originally created in the image of God, is a sort of symbol of the sacred. Engaging with such a human being, who embodies created truth, calls forth truth within us and draws us toward apprehension of, and into relationship with, the Truth beyond us. The word (the symbol for Ricoeur) is only one of the ways the human symbol in the image of God operates. We create visual and musical symbols, and symbols of scent and of taste, for the sacred as well. "God has created us as image-creating creatures and if we neglect this psychic fact we neglect a main stream, a main source of our own religious life," as Ann Belford Ulanov, Jungian analyst, writer, and professor of psychiatry and religion, has written.[14] God addresses us through our engagement with the word "God" and other forms of symbolic expression, as well as through engagement with the human being who is true to creation in the image of God.

By our projections onto the symbol "God" we address ourselves about ourselves and thus, if the image of God were undistorted in us, about God. Beyond the symbol, God really exists. If we were able to be true to God's image, we could perceive God's self-revelation through us and through our symbol "God" to us. We could engage with each other in truth and thereby enter relationship with the Truth beyond us. By our projections, if we were true to the image of God, we could give "God" content that would reveal to us the truth in ourselves and thus to some extent would reveal to us the Truth of Godself. Our projections could not fully reveal God, however, be-cause God is transcendent as well as immanent and thus the Truth of God always exceeds what we can perceive through engagement with any symbol. God does transcend us and is not contained in us, yet

God is revealed in us and in particular in Jesus as our perfection, the realization of the image of God and therefore the true revelation of God.

Our projections could only give content to the symbol that would facilitate God's self-revelation if we could accept God's gift of our goodness as created and thus not distort our creation in the image of God by falling into the brokenness of the adult-child split. The fall, in distorting the image of God in us, however, has also impaired our ability to accept created goodness. I do not suggest that our failure to accept created goodness limits God's ability to reveal Godself, but that our failure to accept our God-proclaimed goodness makes unavoidable our giving content to the symbol that blocks our ability to perceive the ongoing self-revelation of God. Ricoeur says, as noted above, that the removal of projections can restore the symbol as the horizon through which the sacred may draw near.[15] I would add that healing the inner split can restore the human being as the image of God through which God draws near.

Image of God and God are perhaps like lights that shine on and reflect each other, so that, if they are unobstructed, it is difficult to distinguish source from reflection. Light passes back and forth through the "screen" of the symbol "God." The screen is transparent, and even the symbol melts away: God has no name, no graven image. But the invisible, nameless God is a magnet for our projections. Images of our existence, including our unconscious inner splits and repressions, pass like a film in front of the light from the image of God, between image and symbol, and the symbol loses some of its transparency as the light projects those images onto the symbol, as if it were one of the filmy screens used for changes of scenery at the opera on which solid looking "objects" appear and disappear. Backlighting can make the screen transparent even when such "objects" are projected onto it; the divine light behind the symbol can still shine through. But the solid-looking authoritarian father "object" projected out of our existence obscures the light, or we fail to notice the light, being taken in by the apparent reality of the "object" we are projecting.

If we recognize that what we see is our projection, we are not taken in; we do not mistake the "object" for the light, but we know

that as an "object" external to us it is illusory, created by the projection of our inner condition. When we recognize the "object" as our
projection, we see through it, and we see the light, its stream back and
forth to and from the image of God in us unbroken. Then we see that
God is not "Wholly Other" (as Ricoeur says), but intimately connected to us in the truth of our very nature, as created in the image
of God.

The symbol of God as "Father" could be more God-revealing if
human fatherhood were not distorted by a failure radically to accept
created goodness. Then the projected father image would not be a
distortion, because the human father-child relationship would not be
distorted, based on contempt, power, and domination, and there
would not be an inner adult-child split.

Indeed, we probably would not project a father image at all, or
would take more seriously other projections, such as mother, as well.
All images are partial, because each symbol comes from a particular
perspective. Thus each is true: God is father, mother, black, woman,
child—all of these and much more. Created goodness in the image of
God does not mean a static uniformity or a single symbol, but a rich
multitude of goodnesses reflecting all aspects of human reality, including our non-human environment. Each symbol is God-revealing
insofar as it reflects the goodness of God's creation and the acceptance of that goodness in itself and in all creation's other forms.

Our father projection is the one that has captured our attention
and become our idol because it is the one that most obstructs our
vision of God. The contemptuous and authoritarian father is the
illusory "object" on the screen that we have not been able to see
through. The human father (and others in a similar role), split inwardly and outwardly in relation to the child, is the element of our
existence that most fails to flow from creation in the image of God.
Feminist theology has helped us to recognize and begin seeing
through our father projections.

The "Father" model that reflects projections of human fatherhood subject to the adult-child split does contain the child image, as
the human father contains the inner child-self; but, insofar as "God"
is a reflection of our projections, God the Child remains an uncon-

scious aspect of "God," just as the child-self is split off and/or repressed in the human adult. Seeing the image of the father without
consciousness of the inner child-self as "God" is idolatry, because it is
worship of a god revealed through an image other than the true image
of God, through a split and broken humankind. In failing to accept
the God-proclaimed goodness of creation as it is given to us, we fail to
be able to know God and God's goodness.

Although our projections reflect the experience of a humankind
in whom the image of God is distorted, in a sense all works well. The
fact that we project keeps accessible to our consciousness aspects of
ourselves to which we might otherwise lose access. Showing us what
has gone wrong with us, our projections imply what is needed to set
things right and thus point to that in us which is as it was created to
be. Projection itself is part of our created goodness, and it continues to
operate at least potentially to the good. In addition, I believe that
projection is a manifestation of the mutual relationship and mutual
self-revelation between human beings and God. Our projections reveal our distortions not only to us, but also to God.

I have said that the invisible, nameless "God" is a magnet for our
projections, and that God is invisible to us because of our failure to
accept our created goodness. When we fall into brokenness because of
the adult-child split, we fail to be true to our creation in the image of
God, and thus we become unable to perceive God's self-revelation in
ourselves as God's symbol and in our projections onto the symbol
"God." God then is no longer visible to us in creation, no longer
walks with us in the garden. We continue to create symbols and to
project our human condition onto those symbols, and our projections
display our predicament to God clearly enough. But God could resolve our predicament only by becoming visible once more, only by
breaking through the invisibility imposed by our brokenness and again
revealing the divine presence in creation. God became visible to us as
Child in the life, death and resurrection of Jesus, the Christ. God thus
made it clear to us that God's image is still whole in the newborn
human child.

The incarnation bridges the gap between the "God" of our projections and the inner reality of God. God the Child is an aspect of

the inner reality of God, in whose image (Parent, Child, and Spirit) human beings are created. In his fully divine aspect, Jesus is God the Child incarnate, the Christ. In his fully human aspect, Jesus is true to the image of God. In Jesus, the human being, the divine is truly revealed. Because he is the divine Child incarnate and not merely a human being in the image of God, engagement with the truth in Jesus is (and does not merely point toward) engagement with the Truth beyond humankind. And this embodiment of divine Truth comes to us as a human child.

The human existence of Jesus can only be true to creation in the image of God because Jesus is not subject to the fall into the adult-child split. Jesus is not subject to inward splits or repressions and so cannot project anything onto "God" that will obscure God's self-revelation. Not participating in our collective father projections, Jesus is the one human being able both to see our projections for what they are and to see through them. Jesus is the one who sees through the illusory object to the true object, and also sees in our projections onto the symbol "God" what we have revealed about our human condition.

In accordance with the conscious adult aspect of what we project, Jesus uses the name "Father." Although one way of seeing God in the Hebrew Bible is as a paternal figure, "Father" is rarely used as an actual name for God.[16] In the Old Testament, "YHWH," "I am who I am," is the closest thing to a name for God (Ex 3:14). (It is in this image that we are created; in human terms, newly born in the image of God, we are who we are, just as God created us to be.) But Jesus, the incarnate Child, dares to address the first person of the Trinity personally with the name "Father."[17] (Actually, as we have seen in Chapter 7, Jesus addresses "him" as "Abba"—we really should speak of "God the Dada," not "God the Father.")

Jesus sees human father projections for what they are, and in accordance with those projections and in response to being named "Son," he names the "Father." Naming each other, Father and Son reveal their equal status and the mutuality of their relationship: Jesus "called God his own Father, making himself equal with God" (Jn

5:18b). The fact that the naming of both occurs in the context of the life of the incarnate Son reveals, however, that the Childhood of God, not the Fatherhood, is of primary importance for God's self-revelation to us.[18]

Jesus not only gives a name to our father projections, but also gives new content to the paternal symbol.[19] The incarnation corrects our father projections by providing a model of divine Father-Child relationship based on mutuality, wholeness, and unity. It is in relationship with the incarnate Child that the nature of the Father is revealed (see Chapter 7). Revealing God as Child and revealing the Father in relationship with the Child, the incarnation reveals that the inner nature of God is relational.[20] Similarly, the inner nature of our being is relational, adult and inner child-self. The divine Father-Child relationship revealed through the incarnation transforms the traditional model of fatherhood outlined in Chapter 8 into a model of relationship between the incarnate Child, who is God, and a loving, giving, respectful Father, whose nature is revealed in relationship with the Child.

Ricoeur says that culture works the "Father" symbol forward from its archaic roots in our projections toward meaning through love.[21] It seems to me that the gospel, by transforming the authoritarian model into one of mutuality and respect, does work the symbol "Father" forward toward meaning and truth. The problem is that this true working forward is constantly being lost, because the origin of father projections in childhoods shaped by fathers' brokenness, together with the tendency to idealize fathers, gives the model of wrath, punishment, and control a powerful hold. By the time of some later New Testament writings, such as Hebrews 12:5-11 (which borrows from Proverbs 3:11-12), the authoritarian, punitive father model reappears, and the "God" that St. Augustine and Martin Luther portrayed is more closely connected with projections of the punitive fathers of early childhood experience than with the "Abba" to whom Jesus related. Freud speaks of the return of the repressed. Alice Miller speaks of the repeated return of the truth and its repeated repression. The phenomenon of the loss of insight in defense of fathers that

Miller observed in Freud and other psychologists[22] repeats in a different context this loss of the insight manifest in Jesus' relationship with
God the Father and in the gospel revelation that God is Child.

The divine revelation responds to and corresponds with our
inner condition, as creatures in the image of God. I do not suggest
that God became inwardly relational in response to our condition and
our projection of that condition, but that the form in which God
expressed God's preexisting inward relationship in the incarnation
responds to our condition: Human beings characterized the human
being as child in relation to a paternal "God"; and the Word, originally expressed in our creation, was conceived and made flesh as a
human child.

God comprises wholeness in all possible relationships. We see a
paternal "God" through projections of the broken human fatherchild
relationship. Our projection of that broken relationship constellates
the unbroken FatherChild relationship within God, and in the incarnation God manifests wholeness in that relationship to us. The Child
is incarnate as Son, not Daughter, because the human projections that
reveal to God our need for healing are masculine projections.

Divine Father and Son are one God. Jesus, the Son or Child
incarnate, knew God as subject: "I and the Father are one" (Jn
10:30). Similarly, if the human being could be true to creation in the
image of God, there would be unity of subject and object. Symbol
would melt away as God and image of God shed light on each other.
To be true to creation in the image of God accordingly means to cease
to perceive "God" only as object. God as our subject is both the
source and structure of our beingasitis and the power for an existence that organically flows from that source. Image of God is not
totally separated from God; in subjectobject unity the divinehuman
split is healed and once again we can perceive God walking with us in
the garden. Accordingly, Jesus taught us to see Christ in each other.

The inner generative source of the human being, the source of all
aspects of existence, including language, symbol production, and projection, creates the symbol and projects onto it the existence that is
being generated. If that existence is true to the image of God, the

symbol, in mirroring back what is projected, reflects back our inner generative source as outer generative source, "God."

As long as we do not experience God as subject as well as object, we may properly conclude that the "God" we perceive is obscured by our projections. It is through relationship with God the Child and with the inner child-self that we can attain the inner unity that enables us to see through our obscuring projections. These relationships make the experience of subject-object unity possible. Whenever we perceive "God" only "out there," we need to find the connection with what we perceive "in here." There is always an inner connection, because what we perceive is always related to something inside that we project, and because by virtue of our creation in the image of God we always contain and thus project, even if in distorted form, the partial reflection of the God Who Is ("I Am") beyond the symbol.

The revelation of God in the incarnate Child validates the unconscious child-aspect of the "God" of our projections. In terms of our projections, the incarnation is the becoming conscious of the Child aspect of God: God makes visible what may be hidden to human beings due to their inner splits and repressions. The transformed and transforming divine Father-Child relationship of the gospel reveals that distorted inner and outer adult-child relationships are the aspects of human existence to which we must turn our attention with ultimate seriousness.

CHAPTER 11

Letting the Child-Self Heal the Inner Adult-Child Split

> Truly, I say to you, unless you turn and become like children, you will never enter the kingdom of heaven (Mt 18:3).

We have seen in Chapter 3 that when we receive a child in the name of Christ, we receive Christ, God the Child incarnate. The same is true when we receive our own child-selves in the name of Christ. It is our inner child-selves that we must become like if we are ever to enter the kingdom of heaven, the reign of God. The child-self, the child still alive within the adult, is part of the creation that God has called "good." The child-self, reborn in the Spirit and received in Christ's name, is, like the newborn child, the new creation. God the Child is primary for God's self-revelation to us; the child in us is primary for our relationship with God, with self, and with each other in God's reign. If Christ lives in us, the divine Child lives in us. We are required to attend to the child within, approach it as the divine Child. The key to restoring ourselves to our creation in the image of God is true relationship with the inner child-self, the image of God the Child.

I have written of the inner adult-child split, in which the inner child-self is split off and/or repressed. In other words, the adult has rejected as part of the consciously accepted adult identity the early feelings and perceptions that made up a childhood in which adult contempt, and often abuse, made being a child or having a child's feelings seem unacceptable. Some psychologists write of the splitting off and repression of parts of the self, such as feelings of weakness and neediness, or feelings of rage and hatred, both of which are sets of feelings commonly rejected early in abused childhoods. I believe the incarnation reveals the importance of conceiving of a split not of one or more parts, but of the whole child who existed prior to any split. Of course, the whole child is not split off; some aspects (such as rationality) remain and develop into the consciously perceived adult "self." It is the rejection of unwanted memories and feelings that leads to inner splits, and feelings are the key to the wholeness of the child-self. The child who existed, prior to any split, felt intensely all feelings. That whole child still lives within in the potential for fully intense feelings, bridging the splits that psychologists describe.[1]

Christ the Child incarnate is the leaven of wholeness, and wholeness tends to heal brokenness. The resurrection demonstrates that ultimately the power of wholeness is greater than all the forces of human brokenness. The child within, received in the name of Christ, is Christ, the leaven of wholeness. Relating to the wholeness of the child-self means relating to feelings of love and strength and hate and weakness and neediness, as and when each feeling arises, and recog- nizing the unity of the source of all feelings. If we experience all feelings as those of a whole child-self within, this child-self will gradu- ally become a conscious inner object in whom all feelings are inte- grated. The wholeness of the child-self then will be Christ to us, healing our brokenness. By relating to created truth in the child-self, we will become better able to relate to the transcendent Truth that is God.

Split off or repressed feelings that I cannot accept as feelings of my adult self, I can begin to accept as feelings of an inner child-self, to whom I can begin to relate with loving and respectful acceptance. I can begin to want to know all about her and make a commitment to take her feelings seriously. Gradually, through split off and repressed feelings and memories, as they become conscious, she tells me her story. As I accept her and her feelings, I accept my own history, and gradually I integrate my experience of her, my child-self, and begin to know her feelings as my feelings, her story as my story. Through relationship with the emerging wholeness of my child-self, my adult- self grows toward wholeness.

The inner relationship is with the actual individual child of my own childhood, not a symbol or an archetype. To look for possible universal elements in this child would detract from the utter serious-ness with which the individual child or child-self must be treated if healing is to occur. The inner child, like every child, is a real person who needs personal and individual attention. She is not "the child" in the abstract, but this unique child, whom I can know only in the process of relationship with her.

Relationship with the inner child-self is the route to wholeness for the whole self on the model of the relationship of whole Father and whole Child within the unity of Godself.[2] The divine persons each fully manifest wholeness. By internalizing the divine whole-with-whole relational model, the human adult can grow toward wholeness in the inner adult-child relationship. And acceptance of the inner child-self in a relationship of inner care, concern and respect will make possible empathy for all children. The child-self is the seed of wholeness, long buried, which can spring to life in a resurrection from the unconscious and ascension into a greater whole, the whole person, just as the Child, although already whole, rises to take a place in a greater whole, the Godhead itself. The whole human adult, as child of God, takes part too in a larger whole, the whole of creation, redeemed in the reign of God.

Jesus points to the child—to reconciliation with the inner child —as the key to entering or receiving God's reign:

> Truly, I say to you, unless you turn and become like children, you will never enter the kingdom of heaven (Mt 18:3).

> Let the children come to me, do not hinder them; for to such belongs the kingdom of God. Truly, I say to you, whoever does not receive the kingdom of God like a child shall not enter it (Mk 10:14–15).

Martin Luther had other ideas about the meaning of these passages from the gospels. "When Luther looked at his family in 1538, he remarked, 'Christ said we must become as little children to enter the kingdom of heaven. Dear God, this is too much. Have we got to become such idiots?' "[3] He expressed an attitude toward children arising out of the adult-child split, not true relationship with them or with the inner child-self.

Becoming like the child we once were means healing the adult-child split, being once again whole, living in inner relationship with the child-self. Being whole, we would indeed enter the reign of God.

Jesus has told us that the reign of God is in our midst, but entering it never has been easy. Living in relationship with the child-self requires allowing into consciousness and feeling vividly feelings we do not want to feel and have spent our lives avoiding: pain, humiliation, neediness, powerlessness, fear, guilt, rage, and hate, to name a few. It often means becoming conscious too of terrifying and painful memories that lie locked in our unconscious minds. Living in right relationship with the child-self means taking our own childhood feelings and perceptions of reality seriously. Before we can take them seriously, we must have the courage to face them, and we often defend ourselves against them by having contempt for our feelings.

My parents taught me to have contempt for my feelings. By their lack of respect for my feelings, their failure to take my feelings seriously, my parents taught me that my feelings had no significance. My feelings had no impact, did not lead to or justify any action. Therefore I grew up defenseless, unable to act to protect myself, never feeling justified in removing myself from an abusive situation, simply because of my own pain. As long as the abuser continued to demand my presence, I felt that by leaving I would be the one to hurt him. I needed his permission to defend myself.

How easy it is to have contempt for our feelings: "My problems are not so bad. The important thing is not to dwell on them and blow them all out of proportion. I am not one of those people who wallow in their feelings, always dramatizing. They are so self-centered. Can't they see how unimportant their problems are? Think of all the people who are so much worse off. What do I have to feel so bad about? It is better to look on the bright side, count your blessings, think positively. Smile and the world smiles with you. Cry and you cry alone."

Having a balanced picture of reality, acknowledging happy feelings along with unhappy ones, is of course desirable, but misdirected "positive thinking" can be a mask for repression and denial. In my childhood home it was forbidden to speak of anything unpleasant. "No arguments" meant we could never disagree with our father, make any noise, or even try to explain ourselves. Both parents required us to participate in what I have come to think of as the "fantasy of the happy family." It seemed that, if something remained unarticulated, it did not exist. Even if it was said, as when I said, "I hate my brother," its reality could be undone by denial: "You don't mean that; you don't feel that way," or "You (or I) never said that." Thus we had to reject all undesired feelings and perceptions of reality. My father was fond of telling us to "think positively."

Often people who seem to dwell on what we perceive to be negative in reality do not know how to experience freely and appropriately the extremely painful realities behind that negativity. As a victim of abusive positive thinking, I once declared that I was tenaciously negative. Negativity became one of the few ways I could know that I, and reality as I perceived it, existed apart from the family fantasy. Another proof of the reality of my existence was my unhappiness. Unfortunately I did not know how to stop carrying my protective negativity when outside the family circle. My protection became a distorting screen between me and current realities.

As one who has wallowed in my feelings, I believe that wallowing, or the dramatization of feelings, occurs in people who are acting out feelings that they are unable to take seriously in themselves. They at least have some access to their feelings and through them to the painful unknown drama of their lives. A person who wallows or is melodramatic wants to take her or his feelings seriously, but cannot. When others belittle their exaggerated expression of feelings, they receive confirmation of their own doubts as to the legitimacy of their feelings. If someone else takes their feelings seriously rather than treating them with contempt, however, such people may find it possible to begin looking inward seriously and constructively.

In my experience in therapy, in two years with one therapist, the event that was most healing for me was his taking seriously the pain I felt about being hit by snowballs that hostile boys had thrown at me when I was eleven. I related the incident to my therapist long before I had any conscious idea about the abuse I had suffered. I believe my therapist's serious attention to my pain made it possible eventually for me to examine far more difficult issues. His response meant that my pain was real and that I had a right to feel it. For the first time I allowed myself to take my own pain seriously. When others respond to my pain or other feelings with contempt, or belittle my feelings, however, I still become upset and defensive, although now I do not become enraged so easily as I did at one time; I feel my right to my own feelings slipping away, but now consciousness of what is happening helps me to avoid actually losing the feeling and the sense that I have the right to feel it. I may require a little temporary wallowing to get it back!

Too often we may feel that if we take our own feelings and needs seriously we must do so at someone else's expense. Sometimes our parents may have reacted to our feelings and needs as if our feelings would hurt our parents, as if our needs were at the expense of our parents' needs. Others may have told us, and we continue to believe with a sense of shame and guilt, that our feelings are out of proportion or inappropriate. Feeling ashamed and guilty, we try to repress our feelings once more. We deplore "childish" feelings and behavior. We try to distract ourselves: "Concentrate on your work. Go out with friends. Do not dwell on your feelings. Feel better." Sometimes feeling better is not our immediate need. We need to feel our rejected feelings and take them seriously before we can move beyond them and feel better.

In my personal experience, the benefit of psychotherapy has been learning the necessity of trusting who and what I am, including my natural feelings and my perceptions of reality. If my reactions seem inappropriate in the present situation, I must discover when in my past they were appropriate. I must feel the feelings and perceive the underlying reality, or I will never be free to react appropriately in the present. I must undo the effects of the "discipline," humiliations, and abuses of childhood. I must face what seems like the worst in myself. Eschatologically, our end is to be as we truly are. Only God can give the halo.

An early moment of truth along this path came for me when I first realized that I had always asked myself how I ought to feel and tried to feel that way. I had never thought to ask myself how I actually did feel. Beginning to search for my actual feelings, which were largely repressed, was the first step in the long and difficult process toward healing. Rather than existing on the basis of an attitude about myself, I began to live in relationship with myself.

A second, related insight came years later. The woman who was then my therapist helped me to see that what I truly "wanted" was not whatever I happened to think I wanted, but what my feelings told me I wanted. I told her that I had wanted to attend a particular gathering, but on the way there I felt so anxious that I went home instead, and then I felt better. She said I felt better because I had not wanted to go to the gathering. I had thought I wanted to attend, but my feelings revealed the contrary.

The more I come to trust the "me" that God created, the more I find the true, the trustworthy in myself, beyond the feelings and attitudes that seem the worst. It is useless to wonder what human nature is as long as we are caught up in ideas of what it should be. We need to seek not the good but the true in ourselves. The reign of God thus comes not through human progress or development, but through a sort of regress, a movement into ourselves that unties all the knots and lets human being be what it truly is, what God created it to be.

Healing requires feeling fully all the rejected feelings of child-hood and recovering all the repressed perceptions of reality. But this is not easy, because the early experiences were literally unbearable in childhood. The adult-child split did not come about easily or pain-lessly. Breaking one's wholeness is a truly horrible thing to do to oneself. Repression and splitting off of parts of the self are not a mere forgetting of what is painful, but a repudiation of the child-self who felt the unwanted feelings and her or his reality. The inner splitting is an inner act of violence, a psychic suicide. The fuel for the actual split is intense self-hate.

Out of contempt, in their brokenness, adults inflict humiliation, shame, and guilt on children. The child experiences humiliation as coming from an external source, the adult. But because of the rage and hate the experience of humiliation arouses in the child toward the adult, and because of the adult's reaction to the child's aggressive feelings, the child also feels guilt and so may turn the rage and hate against the child's self. The child experiences shame as arising because of an inner defect, and so shame attacks the child's budding core sense of self. Together such feelings lead to the wish to destroy all that brings the feelings on: the imperfections, needs, and weaknesses that seem to attract adult contempt and abuse. Internalizing adult criticism, ridicule, contempt, and abuse, the child suffers intense self-hate and self-destructiveness. Sexual abuse alone is enough to produce this self-hate and the wish to destroy the self.

The child hates whatever parts of the self seem to bring on contempt, humiliation, ridicule, shaming, rejection, neglect, or abuse. These parts of the self tend to center around the child's needs and weaknesses—whatever the child's parents or other adults fail to respect. A child whose needs are not satisfied may be made to feel, for example, that a parent withholds needed attention because of the child's neediness and undesired feelings. The illogical logic the adult seems to suggest is that if only the child did not have so many needs or the feelings that flow in reaction to the frustration of those needs, the needs would be satisfied. The frustration of real needs brings the child pain, anxiety, and anger. The child then wishes to be rid of the needs, both to avoid the feelings and in the hope of obtaining what is needed. The child cannot afford to believe that she or he has the right to expect anything better, to expect anything. The child cannot afford conscious awareness of the reality of a parent who does not satisfy her or his needs, who has contempt for the child or abuses the child. It seems preferable to the child to believe that by controlling herself or himself the child can obtain the desired response and that the adults' failure to respond in the desired way is due to the child's own failure to be perfect. The child hates her or his imperfection.

The child then faces the apparent necessity of psychic suicide, the death of real feelings and perceptions of reality, the death of the soul, for the sake of the only hope, which is illusory, of anything better. The repression of aggressive feelings leaves the child defense-less, and experiences of abuse, as well as the wish to destroy the weak and needy parts of the self, bring fear, the fear of destruction. The abused child experiences the threat of physical and psychic destruc-tion from the abusive adult, ostensibly on account of the child's feel-ings and needs, and the avoidance of that destruction seems to require that the child do the destroying—of those feelings, weaknesses, and needs. The child denies the weakness, the pain, the need, the humil-iation, the shame. The self-hate is too much to endure. The child's sense of self worth is destroyed. The split with the child-self occurs. Identification with adults is consolidated. Unwanted feelings and perceptions of reality are repressed. The child defends against future attacks (external or internal) of ridicule, shaming, and humiliation by shutting them out of consciousness as they occur.

The inner healing process of relationship with the child-self consists of a series of descents into the horrors of the past. The discoveries become successively more devastating, but each descent, if the true significance of feelings and memories is understood, brings greater inner strength and the ability to withstand something worse the next time. Some of the same discoveries are made over and over, but each time in a new way, in greater depth and with greater clarity. Prayer is a constant source of strength and hope.

Eventually this process leads to the reawakening of feelings such as humiliation and shame, the awareness of weaknessess and needs, and finally reactivation of intense self-hate on a conscious level. An inner voice attacks every imperfection, every weakness, every need. The abuse victim feels unworthy of love and would rather be dead. The early crisis is re-engaged, and for healing to occur a new solution must be found. But the old solution continues to present itself as the only way out: "I must reject this weakness, this imperfection, this shame, this need. I must perfect myself, and then I will be lovable." The temptation is to escape into adult accomplishments, the sources, so hard-won in adulthood, of those shreds of self-esteem that now seem to have vanished. In fact, continued successes in adult life forestall this crisis. Failure, the proof of imperfection, is likely to precipitate the crisis, to bring on intense feelings of humiliation, shame, and self-hate. This failure is a gift, because it opens the way to deepest healing. Paradoxically, unaccustomed success or the offer of real acceptance and love may also be a catalyst for the crisis by arousing the abused person's theretofore unconscious feelings of unworthiness.

This crisis is the life or death struggle of the child-self, the struggle that the child could not win the first time, when adult abuses of power made the inner split unavoidable. It is important in this renewed crisis to accept and respect the child-self even in the feeling of self-hate. Like other painful feelings, self-hate is the child-self's message telling what her or his reality was and is. It is very difficult to stand with the child-self and take an inner stand against the self-hate and feeling of worthlessness without taking a stand once again against weakness and neediness. From the child's point of view, the feeling of worthlessness was inseparable from the weakness and neediness, and so the child could not make this distinction. The child tried to resolve the dilemma by banishing weaknesses and needs, but all the child could banish was awareness of them.

The new, healing solution is deceptively simple: to accept and embrace the unavoidable reality of weaknesses, limitations, needs, imperfections. "Courage" is meaningless without weakness, limitation. The greatest courage is required, and yet the imperfection we need to embrace is there all the time. It is part of the human condition. It may seem that accepting this reality should be the easiest thing in the world, but in this crisis it feels like the most difficult because of the illusion that the acceptance of weakness, need, and imperfection will mean the permanent loss of the hope of fulfilled needs. It seems to mean accepting that one truly is worthless and unlovable. In fact, however, only embracing the reality of one's own imperfection, need, and weakness can lead to real hope of need fulfillment. This inner acceptance does not come all at once; it too is a process. But breaking a previously unconscious identification with the inner voices of contempt and self-hate by recognizing them and consciously accepting the idea of personal imperfection begins a process that, surprisingly quickly, begins to bring signs of new life.

All that I have related as the abused child's experience has been my experience. Others may experience the process differently. The imperfections that I must embrace include my femaleness, which I have experienced as imperfection because of the abuse and rejection I suffered as a girl. To move deeper in respectful relationship with my child-self, LJ, to embrace her weaknesses and needs and her female-ness, is finally to love her. This love is the only overcoming of self-hate, the healing once and for all of the inner adult-child split. If I love LJ, then I love myself. The inner gesture of healing means forgiving myself for being human and for being female. It means knowing both my strengths and my limitations, as woman, as God's creature. In fact, my strengths may be among the "weaknesses" (for a female child) that I had to reject and now can love. Now I can feel that I have the right to expect something better, the hope of having my real needs satisfied. I do not have to be perfect to be loved. My only human perfection is as a limited creature of God, complete with weaknesses and needs.

The crucifixion and resurrection mirror the healing process and provide a model of inner adult-child unity and wholeness, in terms of both Jesus' inner human adult-child relationship and God's inner Father-Child relationship. Human fathers who were broken, split inwardly from their child-selves, crucified the Son, not understand-ing the significance of God the Child. The fathers acted not in mutu-ality but out of broken human values and attitudes, judging and pun-ishing Jesus. Jesus' authenticity and integrity as a whole human being made his death inevitable. His wholeness attracted all the forces of brokenness, which tends to break wholeness. Therefore the gift of his life was also a sacrifice entailing his death. Similarly, the God-given wholeness of every child is broken, a sacrifice to the brokenness of adults.

Jesus accepted the humbling experience of death on a cross:

Have this mind among yourselves, which is yours in Christ Jesus, who, though he was in the form of God, did not count equality

with God a thing to be grasped, but emptied himself, taking the
form of a servant, being born in the likeness of men. And being
found in human form he humbled himself and became obedient
unto death, even death on a cross (Phil 2:5-8).

Jesus related the idea of humbling to the child: "Whoever humbles
himself like this child, he is the greatest in the kingdom of heaven"
(Mt 18:4). Jesus requires our humbling ourselves like a child, not
exalting ourselves by assuming godlike status: "For every one who
exalts himself will be humbled, and he who humbles himself will be
exalted" (Lk 14:4).

Mary and the other women in the gospels exhibited the humility
that Jesus urged, but Jesus had to teach the male disciples to serve
others, not to lord it over them (Mk 10:35-45). A woman, in contrast to men, would wash Jesus' feet with her hair (Jn 11:2) or anoint
his head (Mk 14:3-9). The Syrophoenician woman accepted humiliation for the sake of her child (Mk 7:24-30). Unlike the male disciples, the women followers of Jesus did not run away from his humiliating death but remained at the cross. Perhaps they could face his
pain and humiliation because such feelings were a more integrated
part of their experience. The Greek word in the New Testament that
is translated "disciple" means "one who is taught." Perhaps the men
who followed Jesus were called "disciples" because they needed to be
taught so much.

In our era, parents have more readily tolerated pain and weakness
in daughters than in sons. And, unlike sons, daughters cannot escape
their humiliating status simply by growing up. Sons, indeed, are
brought up to take their place as fathers, while daughters have usually
been brought up, in our culture, to remain subordinate, perpetually
childlike in relation to their fathers, brothers and husbands, and even
to their sons. Jesus preached humility to men who had power and
status.

Jesus' suffering in the crucifixion is the model of truly experiencing powerlessness, pain and humiliation. Chapter 23 of Luke relates
that Jesus was treated with contempt and was mocked; although
innocent, he was crucified with criminals; he was scoffed at and again

mocked. Matthew too relates, in chapter 27, that Jesus was mocked, spat upon, derided, reviled and crucified. According to Mark 14, Jesus was sorrowful, betrayed, forsaken, sworn against by false wit-nesses, silent before his accusers, accused of blasphemy, condemned, spat upon, struck, subjected to blows, and denied by one of his closest followers. In Mark 15, Jesus was accused; a murderer was released rather than he; he was envied, crucified, scourged, forced to wear a purple cloak and a crown of thorns, struck, spat upon, treated with mock homage, mocked, stripped, derided, again mocked, reviled and forsaken.

It was in the context of such humiliation and suffering, as Jesus died, that a centurion perceived that Jesus was the Son of God (Mk 15:39). Divine Sonship was revealed upon his death in the midst of the very feelings that abuse arouses in children and forces them to split off and/or repress, thereby rejecting their child-selves.

The earthly failure of Jesus is the gift that makes possible our healing. Our love for Jesus, and the fact that his divine Sonship is revealed in the crucifixion, open for us the possibility of empathizing with his pain, humiliation, and other feelings. The crucifixion thus can open the way to our own long rejected feelings. We may experi-ence the crucifixion accounts differently from other stories of suffer-ing and humiliation because as Christians we can experience Jesus' life as ours, as Paul did: "It is no longer I who live, but Christ who lives in me" (Gal 2:20). To take up one's cross and follow Jesus could mean to follow him into such feelings. In fact, the crucifixion may be the moment of divine revelation precisely because in encountering the Child on the cross we can encounter our own split-off pain and humiliation and thereby the child within can rise from entombment in the unconscious to a new life of wholeness with the Child.

To rise with Christ requires us to become again as we were as little children, to relive the experience emotionally and become truly alive again, a new creation born of the Spirit. But reliving the child-hood experience is painful. According to Paul,

> When we cry, "Abba! Father!" it is the Spirit himself bearing witness with our spirit that we are children of God, and if chil-

dren, then heirs, heirs of God and fellow heirs with Christ, pro-
vided we suffer with him in order that we may also be glorified
with him (Rom 8:15b–17).

Not even bodily injury destroys the human spirit if the victim
can know what is being done and can experience and express all the
reactive feelings with an empathic listener.[4] "And do not fear those
who kill the body but cannot kill the soul; rather fear him who can
destroy both soul and body in hell" (Mt 10:28). For too many children crucifixion means the distortion of reality (e.g. "it's for your own
good"[5]) and the denial of feelings in addition to outright abuse—the
destruction of the soul as well as injury to the body.[6] Yet the resurrection of Jesus, the Child, reveals that wholeness is ultimately stronger
than brokenness. Crucifixion means potential resurrection; split-off
and repressed feelings always press toward expression, and the truth
always presses toward consciousness. However hard we may try to
kill the child within, the child lives. The tomb cannot contain
the Child.

The Father respects the Child and accepts all the Child's feelings, even despair and anger at the Father. Feeling that the Father has
forsaken him (Mk 15:34; Mt 27:46), Jesus feels the same despair as all
children whose fathers (or mothers) abandon them or do not prevent
their suffering. Adults do fail children, sometimes unavoidably. Even
abandonment, suffering, and humiliation are sometimes unavoidable
(and certain kinds of frustrations may become increasingly appropriate as the child matures).[7] The Father-Child relationship reveals
that the Child is free to have these feelings and that the Father does
not reject the Child because of them. The Child does not have to be
perfect, free of weaknesses and needs, or a success in worldly terms, to
deserve the Father's love. The Father still loves the Child and raises
the Child up. Since the Child is free to feel and to fail without risking
loss of the Father's respect and love, the Child and the Father are
reconciled quickly.

It might seem, however, that the Father's abandonment of the
Son was avoidable and that the Father should have saved the Son
from the need to suffer. Otherwise, how can we assert that the Fa-

ther-Child relationship heals and transforms the human adult-child relationship? God is at the same time Father and Son. It seems to me that in the crucifixion God is so completely identified with the Child, with human weakness, powerlessness, and neediness, that in a sense there is no separate powerful Father who can do anything to stop the Son's suffering. The consciousness of Father and Son is one. At the same time as God is totally in the Child, God is totally in the human condition, wholly God and wholly human. Thus God fully shared our human condition. Yet Father and Son remained distinct persons. The Father's identification with the Son incarnate in the crucifixion might be like the feeling a mother has of being one with her newborn child, knowing the child's pain and need from the inside.[8] When the child suffers, the mother loses her consciousness of being separate from her baby. The mother thus enters into the child's helplessness, although she also remains mother. In the instant when she feels the child's pain and need, she is helpless. Only in emerging from the need as a consciously separate person can the mother provide for the child's need. The momentary parent-child merger of consciousness is perhaps prolonged in the crucifixion. In feeling the Child's suffering and humiliation, the Father feels the human condition in all its brokenness. On Jesus' death, the Father's separateness again becomes conscious, and the power of God then raises Jesus, the Child incarnate, from the tomb and restores his life.

The crucifixion reveals that God the Child is God identified with weakness, not with power over those who are weaker. The crucifixion and resurrection mirror powerlessness positively and thus make possible the integration of feelings that arise in the abused person. The male disciples avoided and denied the passion predictions, refusing to accept the need for Jesus to suffer and die. They could not respect a savior who exhibited such weakness, who was destined to fail in worldly terms.

But Jesus tells his followers to take up their own crosses and follow him (Mk 8:34). People who refuse their own pain, who do not take up their own crosses, will inevitably cause others pain. Thus the suffering servant, like many a child, had to bear the torment denied by others:

> Surely he hath borne our griefs and carried our sorrows; yet we
> esteemed him stricken, smitten by God, and afflicted. But he was
> wounded for our transgressions, he was bruised for our iniquities;
> upon him was the chastisement that made us whole, and with his
> stripes we are healed (Is 53:4–5).

Jesus did not refuse his own pain; he bore it, and the fathers' in the
process, and thus made possible the breaking of the cycle of adult-
child splits and the concomitant cycle of abuse.

It is difficult to maintain consciousness of the message of the
cross. The movement away from consciousness of Jesus' suffering
began even as the gospels were being written. The earliest authors,
Paul and Mark, focused on the crucifixion as the moment of revelation of the divinity of Christ. Matthew, however, was more concerned with the event as a fulfillment of scripture; Luke's emphasis
was the innocence of Jesus; and for John the lifting up of Jesus onto
the cross was exaltation. Some of the later reformers removed the
crucified Jesus from the cross as a symbol for worship and rejected the
real presence of Christ in the eucharist. They attempted to remove
consciousness of the reality of Jesus' suffering from both the Lord's
supper and the cross.

An ordained minister told me when I was a child that the cross
is empty because Christ is risen. We celebrated Easter but did not
observe Good Friday: It would not do to dwell on all that unpleasant-
ness. Better to tidy things up, not be morbid. This particular brand of
Protestantism thus furthered the denial and repression of unwanted
feelings and lessened the possibility of transformation. I believe that
the reality of suffering portrayed in the crucifix and the real presence
of Christ in the eucharist are the aspects of Roman Catholic worship
that most attracted me to conversion. I had never understood the
meaning of Jesus or of holy communion. In becoming Catholic I
became Christian for the first time.

The eucharist and the crucifix say: Take suffering seriously.
Because Christ lives in me, he is my right to take my own suffering
seriously. If I can take my experiences and my feelings seriously, then
and only then can I be free from the past and rise to a new life. Only
then can I avoid inflicting my suffering on others.

The presence of Christ in communion is real. Christ the Word is really wholeness, really given to us as leaven for our wholeness. We must be open to receive that leaven, accept the real presence, engage with it fully, take it in. In the mass we see once again that our brokenness breaks Christ's wholeness, but the resurrection reveals that brokenness ultimately cannot prevail. In us as a community, as members of the body of Christ, he can become whole again; we reconstitute his wholeness as he constitutes our wholeness. In relationship with the child-self, as in the eucharist, we relive past suffering that is a living reality, for the sake of healing, of wholeness.

CHAPTER 12

Honor and Forgive?

HONOR YOUR FATHER AND YOUR MOTHER

There will never be a liberation of children in this world unless adults enter relationship with their child-selves and find healing for their inner adult-child splits. In fact, it is the child-self who heals the adult. As we have seen in Chapter 11, healing the inner adult-child split requires feeling fully the repressed feelings of childhood and recovering childhood perceptions of the circumstances in which those feelings arose. Some of those feelings are very painful—such feelings as fear, sorrow, despair, self-hate, guilt, humiliation, weakness, and helplessness.

There are other feelings, however, that bring a different kind of pain. These are the aggressive feelings. Taking up one's cross and following Jesus must mean giving up the idealization of the parents of childhood, going all the way to the death of the idealized childhood and descending into the hell of feelings such as rage and even hate toward the parents of childhood. A realistic appraisal of the parents of childhood can occur only when both painful feelings and reactive rage and hate are consciously owned. I have written in Chapter 6 of my personal difficulty in feeling and acknowledging to myself my hate toward my abuser. Hating one's parent is almost unbearable for an adult. It seems unavoidable that children would repress or split off these feelings, even if parents did not forbid their expression.

It seems that healing the inner adult-child split means creating a new "split" from one's parents. The new "split" from the idealized parents of childhood is not an intrapsychic split such as the splitting off of feelings in childhood that instituted the inner adult-child split,

105

but a conscious separation and individuation from the parents whose contempt and abuse caused the original inner split. The new "split" thus is inwardly integrating rather than disintegrating.

The healing process is not cheap. It costs dearly. It involves awful deaths and truths and intense pain. Feelings that a child was denied the right to feel, or could not bear to feel, are intense and frightening and painful, and they tell stories we do not want to hear about parent-child "love" and just how broken and distorted human relationships in this world often really are. Victims of an abusive upbringing prefer to hang onto the belief that, whatever our parents did to us, it was for our own good, not that it is part of the fabric of the fall itself.

Jesus acknowledges the cost of living out the gospel of God the Child and taking the child-self seriously.

> Do not think that I have come to bring peace, but a sword. For I have come to set a man against his father, and a daughter against her mother, and a daughter-in-law against her mother-in-law; and a man's foes will be those of his own household. He who loves father or mother more than me is not worthy of me; and he who loves son or daughter more than me is not worthy of me; and he who does not take his cross and follow me is not worthy of me (Mt 10:34-42).

At times, however, Jesus quotes approvingly the commandment to honor father and mother (see Mt 15:4-7; 19:19; Mk 7:10-13; 10:19; Lk 18:20), although even then he seems to try to push people past the traditional commandment to a new understanding. How can victims of childhood contempt and abuse understand the commandment to honor parents who have so injured them and aroused such reactive feelings of rage and hatred in them? How can we honor our parents and still take our child-selves seriously?

The wording of the commandment is instructive:

> Honor your father and your mother, that your days may be long in the land which the Lord your God gives you (Ex 20:12).

God does not command us to honor our parents that we may please God, or that we may enter God's reign, or that we may be whole human beings, but "that your days may be long in the land which the Lord your God gives you." Given a fallen world, this is certainly practical advice. The child who openly expresses hostile reactive feelings to parents or cries in pain and need may well not have days that are long in this world. With increasing frequency abuse is identified as a cause of severe injury or even death to infants and children. Yet, in general, it is the child whose aggression is feared, not the parents:

> The idea behind the commandment is that it is better to inculcate a positive norm of conduct than to threaten crude outbursts of hate and contempt with the direst penalties. The question whether the father is worthy of respect is silenced by the impressive nature of the divine command.[1]

Today humankind as a whole faces the possibility that our days in the land God gives us may draw to a close. If Miller is correct that the cause of such destructiveness as drug abuse, environmental pollution, and the threat of nuclear war has roots, even in part, in adult contempt for weakness and the discharge in adulthood of displaced childhood rage and other reactive feelings,[2] then the original commandment is no longer adequate advice. Miller points out that we lack a commandment saying: "Honor your children so that they will be able to honor others as well as themselves."[3] In John's gospel, Jesus does say, "He who does not honor the Son does not honor the Father who sent him" (Jn 5:23). I suggest, in addition, that the following would be appropriate: Honor your children that the days of humankind may be long in the earth that God has given us. We can no longer afford accommodation to a fallen world. We must become like children and enter the reign of God if we are to survive at all.

If we are to continue to take the scriptural commandment seriously, who are the parents we are to honor? Jesus asked, when told that his mother and brothers sought him,

> "Who are my mother and my brothers?" And looking around on those who sat about him, he said, "Here are my mother and my

brothers! Whoever does the will of God is my brother, and sister, and mother" (Mk 3:33–35).

Jesus did not mention his father, perhaps because he honored God the Father alone as his father. Among human beings Jesus honors those who do God's will. A parent who plays god, who tries to recreate a child in the parent's image of goodness, who has contempt for a child's smallness and weakness, who uses or abuses a child, who causes a child to reject the child-self with its feelings and perceptions of reality, is not one who does the will of God.

Ultimately, we are judged from the viewpoint of the child: the Child will return to judge us all. "For with the judgment you pronounce you will be judged, and the measure you give will be the measure you get" (Mt 7:2). It is the Son, not the Father, who has come to bring a sword (Mt 10:34). "The Father judges no one, but has given all judgment to the Son, that all may honor the Son" (Jn 5:22). The child who sees through abusive treatment, or who has not been abused, lied to and manipulated, has an innate sense of truth, justice, and fairness. Children naturally see through phoniness and injustice, but they are relatively powerless. Their viewpoint has final reality, however, even where oppression has taken away their ability to judge for themselves. Each of us is judged by the child-self within, particularly if the child-self is unconscious. Abusive parents are judged by the violence, self-destructiveness and/or emotional disturbances of their children, and often by the cycle of child abuse passed on to their grandchildren. All adults are judged collectively by the sexual abuse and battering of children, the hunger and homelessness of children, the imprisonment of children (such as illegal aliens), and the suicide of teenagers in our own country, by the starvation of children in Africa and elsewhere, by the gassing and burning of children in Nazi Germany.

Having discovered what my parents did to me and having felt all the attendant feelings, including hate toward them, how can I honor them? Do I honor them by protecting them, keeping silent, continuing the pretense of untroubled "love"? Do I honor them by being honest with them for the first time, breaking, shattering the illusions we have all lived by, only to find that their illusions are unshatterable, that their systematic denial and rewriting of history is so profound and pervasive that all I can do is risk losing again my own sense of reality about what happened to me if I try to deal with them in terms of "truth"? Do I continue to stay away, a form of protecting them from my feelings, but also of protecting myself so that I can at least maintain a sense of reality and not be cast back into the insane system of my childhood?

Having found the truth from my child-self's point of view, I must be true to that truth. I cannot go on pretending, and I will not risk losing my hard-won sense of reality. Perhaps I honor my parents by doing the best I can to get my life on a better track, to relive those dreadful feelings and move on from them, like the wind blowing where it will, not knowing where this new birth of the Spirit will take me. I can accept that my particular parents now do not wish me ill, whatever their ambivalence toward me may have been during my childhood. They do want my well-being. Perhaps I honor them by becoming as happy and creative as I can be, in the only way I can, even if the healing process disrupts my ability to relate to them, temporarily or even permanently. I do not want to hate my parents; hate is incredibly painful. I do not want their denials to shut me out of the family. But how can I dishonor my parents by owning my feelings, my perceptions of reality, my whole self? How do I dishonor them by letting God have God's way in having created me to be who I am? In this way surely I honor those who carried out God's wish to give me life.

I am not justified in blaming my parents in a way that enables me to avoid responsibility for my own harmful actions. Whatever my parents did to me, it is part of me now, and, just as in a sense they could not help inflicting on me the consequences of their own upbringing, I cannot help but inflict on others the consequences of what they did to me, until I consciously reexperience my childhood feelings in their appropriate context. Then and only then I will not be in danger of displacing my childhood rage and inflicting it on others, such as children, minority groups, the poor, or myself. I am as responsible for my actions as my parents were for their actions toward me.

Human brokenness does not absolve us of responsibility; our fallen state does not take away our responsibility for sin.

If I act out my childhood feelings toward my parents in the present, I am not reexperiencing them appropriately. My aged parents are now weaker than I am. Acting out my childhood rage and hate in relation to them now would be as much a manifestation of displaced aggression as if I inflicted my rage and hate onto my own children. Entering into my child-self is an intrapsychic process, an experience of early feelings in relation to the internalized parents of childhood, not the abuse of my present-day parents. Like God in the incarnation, I must place myself with those who are weaker and less powerful, even if those persons are the same parents who abused me when they were the more powerful ones. This does not mean that I may not confront them with the truth of the feelings and perceptions that I discover, however. And if they continue to abuse me emotionally with their contempt and their denials, I have a right and a responsibility to myself to put a stop to their behavior, if necessary by refusing to communicate with them.

> Truly, I say to you, there is no one who has left house or brothers or sisters or mother or father or children or lands, for my sake and for the gospel, who will not receive a hundredfold now in this time, houses and brothers and sisters and mothers and children and lands, with persecutions, and in the age to come eternal life. But many that are first will be last, and the last first (Mk 10:29–31).

AS WE FORGIVE THOSE WHO TRESPASS AGAINST US

None of us is without sin; we all need forgiveness, and as Christians we pray for God's forgiveness "as we forgive those who trespass against us." But when we have recovered feelings such as hatred toward the parents of our childhood, who may have abused us severely, how can we forgive them?

Jesus offers a model for forgiveness that can help us to move beyond discovery and acceptance of the facts, feeling hatred, and the desire for revenge. In Luke 23:34, the crucified Jesus prays, "Father, forgive them; for they know not what they do." Jesus, the Child incarnate, can see the tragedy of the crucifying fathers' position: "They know not what they do." Jesus can see through what they are doing to him. Unlike the crucifying fathers, Jesus is not blinded by the adult-child split and adult rationalizations for the abuse of children, including adult attitudes about the evil in children. The fathers relied on similar rationalizations in ordering the death of Jesus. Children cannot forgive, or ask God to forgive, their parents, if they are unable to know what was done to them or why.[4] The Son can see what neither human fathers nor their children can see, that the fathers are both abusing creation and attacking Godself in crucifying the Child. The fathers do not know what they are doing because they in turn were denied the right to feel their feelings or to know the nature of what was being done to them in childhood. As a result, they cannot empathize with the Son.

Forgiveness is always available to the crucifying fathers, however, even if they do not acknowledge their crucifying role to themselves or to the child, because Jesus, the Child, sees the truth and freely asks Abba, "Forgive them." The forgiveness of God, Father and Child, means that God is always open to reconciliation, even with those who crucify Jesus, if only they can face the truth about their actions and accept the offer of reconciliation.

As a victim of the adult-child split I contain not only a child who suffers with the Child at the hand of the fathers, but also a father who cries with the fathers, "Crucify her!" To the extent that I unconsciously identify with powerful parental introjects in rejection of the powerless inner child, making impossible empathy with the weakness and neediness of myself or others, I crucify the Child. Getting in touch with my child-self's rage, helplessness, and self-hate means that I must also break the identification with the parents of childhood. I remain the crucified child because I am also the crucifying parent. When I discover my inner parents from my inner child's point of view, as crucifying fathers, and consciously experience their abuse and contempt and my resulting self-hate in the inner urge to

crucify the child, crucifying father and crucified child can stand face
to face within me in mutual relationship, and true self-respect can
begin. The father can acknowledge: I have crucified you. Forgive me.
The child can experience the respect in this encounter and shed the
humiliation of the past. Yes, I forgive you. The child is released from
the cross and looks the father in the eye as an equal. My personal
power is released from maintaining splits and repressions and becomes
available to me as creative psychic energy.

The crucifixion need not go on forever. The crucifixion is for
healing; we must feel our pain and other feelings because they are real,
but suffering is not an end in itself. I learned this vividly when a
spiritual director asked me in what way I related to Jesus most deeply.
When I told her I related most deeply to Jesus on the cross, she asked
me to meditate on the crucifixion and see what Jesus had to say to me
there. When I did so, I was alarmed to encounter an intensely angry
Jesus, who roared at me, "Let me down from this cross!" After feeling
fear at Jesus' anger, I realized that, in focusing only on Jesus' suffering,
weakness, and death, I had denied his great power and strength—the
very power and strength that enabled him to face his suffering and
death. I was horrified to find a voice in me that cried, "Crucify him!
Crucify the Child!" It was time for me to see how I kept the Child,
and my child-self, on the cross. It was time to face the crucifying
father in myself. The adult-child split occurred in me when I accepted my parents' contemptuous view of me as a child and came to
hate and reject myself. They thus became part of my psychic makeup,
the inner crucifiers of my child-self. Before my child-self could forgive
my parents, the internal crucifiers had to stop crucifying, to let her
down off the cross. I was both crucifier and crucified, and it was time
to put a stop to the inner crucifixion.

Christianity offers more than crucifixion and mourning a past
that can never be changed.[5] On the third day the mourners found
Jesus' tomb empty! The resurrection and ascension of the Child mean
that the past, experienced and not denied, can be overcome. As Parent, God is sensitive to our needs as no human parent (or therapist)
can be. As we relate to God "like a child," God relates back to us as
Parent and corrects the injuries of childhood. My projections onto

the symbol "God" reflect some of my experiences of my own parents: overwhelming, demanding, punitive, perfectionistic; yet, in relation-ship with God, if I am open and really engage with God, I experience God's love, acceptance, respect, and empathy. We bring what we have to God, and through relationship with us God transforms what we bring and gives it back to us as nourishment, as gift, as what we really need.

Through this healing relationship, in time God makes it possible for me to consent to the forgiveness that God freely gives my parents, for I no longer suffer any lack for which I feel the need to hold my parents responsible. The "I" who give this consent must comprise my child-self as well as my adult-self. My child-self heals me as I take her feelings with absolute seriousness and accept them as my feelings. My child-self is the source of the new "split" from the parents of my childhood, and she must also be the source of any consent to forgive-ness that heals this "split."

Forgiveness is an openness to reconciliation that may occur when there is no longer any inner obstacle to reconciliation, when the truth is known and fear and the desire for revenge are laid to rest. Forgiveness is a gift of God, by grace. God forgives, is open to recon-ciliation, because God does not want any of us to be excluded from God's reign. Ultimately, when my longing for reconciliation with God and with all humankind is greater than my longing for revenge; when my love for God's reign exceeds my hate for those who have injured me, I too can be open to their reconciliation and pray with Jesus for their forgiveness—for they knew not what they did.

Beyond the emergence of the pain, need, powerlessness, rage, hate, and self-hate of the child-self, the strength and possibility of the child I once was also begin to emerge. For while weakness, need, and imperfection are part of the human condition, feelings of powerless-ness are reactive—to the exercise of adult power over the child. Heal-ing means that where the oppressive father and crucified child have lived their split existence in place of our real selves, instead Christ the Son, who is the free expression of our real selves, will live in relation-ship with the loving divine Abba. The child-self is the route to a pre-existing power in oneself that is not a power over those who are weaker, but a power to be in the image of God and to exist authentically and creatively out of that being. God the Child is my redeemer. My child-self, received in Christ's name, is Christ, God the Child incarnate. Relationship with the Child/child-self heals all splits, inner and outer.

After I had written most of the above portions of this chapter, my pastor asked me to speak on the "First Word" on Good Friday. The "First Word" is, of course, "Father, forgive them, for they know not what they do." At first I prepared a nice, safe talk, but I knew that I was not being true to LJ, my child-self. I felt that God was calling me to dig deeper into my own issues concerning forgiveness.

Almost exactly two years earlier, on Holy Thursday, I had first recovered a memory of being sexually abused. That Holy Week, at the Easter Vigil, was also the time of my entry into full communion with the Roman Catholic Church. The week was fraught with emotional highs and lows. Then, after struggling for about four months to deal with my discovery (see Chapter 6), I decided to join my family for a week's vacation at the seashore. My sense of reality about the memory of abuse was wearing thin—I was inclined to think it was all my imagination—and I thought I might learn something if I spent time with my parents. And I did not want to be left out.

I did indeed learn a great deal during that week at the beach. I could not tolerate being near my father even for a short time. I forced others to rearrange themselves at the dinner table so that I would not have to sit near him. Fortunately, the group and the house were large enough to make a certain amount of evasion possible. My feelings, however, were struggling to emerge, and my avoidance of contact with my father actually served the avoidance of consciousness of my feelings. Being unable to cope with the situation alone and feeling unable to talk with family members about what was happening, I fell into a strangely familiar sense of isolation from the rest of the family. My misery increased until finally my brother-in-law offered to take me for a drive and asked how I was feeling. I said, "I feel like screaming." He told me to go ahead, and I did, loud and long. This helped to break loose the intense rage and hate that had been buried for so many years. I began to have fantasies of murdering my father in the most horrible possible ways. I have not seen my father since that week nearly three years ago. I refused to permit him to telephone me, because of the feelings his calls aroused. I felt numb during each call, and afterward I felt invaded. I felt a compelling need to "keep him out."

I felt possessed by hate and rage until the following Lent. I had known that I would have to go through the feelings that had been repressed, but they wore me out. Hate was more painful than any feeling I had felt up to that time. (Humiliation, accompanied by rage, came later, and it may have been worse.) And I could not seem to let go of the hate, or rather I felt as if it would not let go of me. Then, during the last week of Lent, I wondered how I would be able to celebrate Easter in such an emotional state. I prayed that the Lenten season itself would offer me some help, and it did. I realized that I could not get rid of my hate, but that I could only descend all the way to a sort of death in it. Fighting the feeling did not help. I had to give myself to it utterly and go all the way to the bottom of it, trusting that after this "death" there would be a resurrection. There was. In a sense my Good Friday and Easter Sunday came early. The feeling of hate intensified to the point where it burned itself out. The potential to feel hate for my father may still be in me, but I have felt it only fleetingly in the last two years.

And so another year passed, and I was preparing to speak on the "First Word." Although I was no longer consumed by hate, I knew that I had not forgiven my father. I did not think I could, or that anyone should expect me to forgive him. But God, through my pastor, called me to face this most difficult issue more directly and in greater depth than I had before. The following is the talk I delivered on Good Friday last year. I received the criticism that the talk was too abstract, not personal enough, but I was not prepared then to make my personal stake in the question more clear in so public a way.

———————— ৡ৵ ————————

"Father, forgive them, for they know not what they do." Jesus spoke this prayer as he suffered on the cross. Jesus was innocent, yet he was able to pray for the forgiveness of those who humiliated and killed him. Sometimes we, like Jesus, may be innocent victims. Can we do what Jesus did? Can we pray for the forgiveness of those who have wronged us?

What about the victims of racism, of sexism, of unjust economic structures; the victims of violence, of rape, of child abuse? How can they forgive? How can a girl who has been sexually abused by her father forgive him? How can she be expected to?

But Jesus taught us to pray, "Forgive us our trespasses as we forgive those who trespass against us." Is God's forgiveness conditioned on our forgiving? If so, is the victim then thrown into the wrong, made guilty by the inability to forgive? Or is Jesus' forgiveness of the crucifiers beyond the capability of ordinary human beings? If forgiveness is required of us, how are we to understand what it means to forgive?

When it comes to being forgiven, in the sacrament of reconciliation, we learn that God has already forgiven us, and we become reconciled with the community as well as with God and with ourselves. Forgiveness and reconciliation thus are connected, but they are not the same thing. To say that God has already forgiven us means that God is always open to reconciliation with us, even knowing the truth about us. In God, there is no obstacle to reconciliation—no fear, no failure to see the truth, no bearing a grudge, no insistence on revenge. Reconciliation occurs as soon as we face the truth of our situation, acknowledge how we have broken relationship with ourselves, with each other, and with God, and genuinely desire to change. There can be no real reconciliation without facing this truth. Confession is not a condition on God's forgiveness; facing the truth is simply part of what reconciliation is. God is truth, and all reconciliation among us is also reconciliation with God.

Looking at how God forgives us, it seems to me, surprisingly, that we ordinary mortals can forgive, with the help of God's healing forgiveness and love. God's forgiveness is an offer of reconciliation that we can accept at any time. The offer is never withdrawn. To forgive does not mean that we take on responsibility for making reconciliation happen. It means that we, like God, are open to reconciliation, and that we are willing to be used as God's instruments for reconciliation. God loves us and wants all of us to be reconciled in the reign of God. For us, to forgive means that we are willing to be with those who have wronged us in a redeemed creation. It does not necessarily mean that we will be in intimate relationship with them, but that we are willing for them to be reconciled. By refusing to forgive, we think that we can hold wrongdoers apart, deny them reconciliation. But actually we have no control over their reconciliation. Only God can grant or deny reconciliation to the sinner. If we are unable to forgive, we maintain division; we are not reconciled.

I sometimes think that entering God's reign is like being invited to a banquet and being asked to take a place beside the people I least want to be near in the whole world. It means recognizing that if God has accepted them and loves them, if they are reconciled to God, then I have nothing to hold against them. If I refuse to sit beside them at God's banquet, if I refuse to enter God's reign because they are there, then I am the one who is not reconciled to God.

If we are unable to forgive, unwilling to be open to reconciliation with those who have injured us, we ourselves need God's loving, healing forgiveness, which gives us the courage to face the truth and be open to reconciliation. Just as the wrongdoer must face the truth before reconciliation is possible, so the call to forgive means that we also have a responsibility to discover the truth, both of what has happened to us and of our inner obstacles to forgiveness. As victim, we may fall prey to self-doubt about the reality of what happened to us, or dwell on feeling guilty about not being able to forgive, because it would be more difficult to accept an unthinkable truth. We may seek "reconciliation" that is really a lie as long as the truth is not known and acknowledged on both sides. Forgiving does not mean denying reality or buying into someone else's denial.

And true reconciliation does not exclude our feelings. Feeling anger, even hatred, in response to what has been done to us is not a refusal of relationship or of truth. Feelings are the stuff relationship is made of. Real feelings are part of the truth. Reconciliation means the restoration of relationship in which feelings can be expressed and respected, in which problems can be faced and worked through. It is for nothing less than the kingdom of God that we must face the worst, feel the painful hate, even the desire for revenge, and go all the way to the bottom of those feelings and die to them and in them.

We are required to forgive, not to make the victim guilty instead of the wrongdoer; not to forget what happened, or pretend it's all right, or even to let them off the hook. The responsibility to forgive is not specifically a responsibility to those who wronged us, but to God and to the whole community and to ourselves—to the hope of reconciliation for all of us in God's reign.

Similarly, being forgiven is not just for our own benefit, but also for the reconciliation of all of us. Therefore, we also have a responsibility to accept forgiveness, to acknowledge how we have broken relationship, and to come to reconciliation.

For forgiving and being forgiven have the same purpose: reconciliation, healing, the restoration of the original harmony of creation, the reign of God. As the one wronged, we participate, however innocently, in a rupture in creation. Thus when we have been wronged we share responsibility with the one who has wronged us to let God heal the rupture in creation through us. Individual divisions do matter; a fabric full of tiny tears will disintegrate.

Forgiving does not mean reconciling ourselves to the wrong that has been done, nor to the injury we have suffered, but exactly the opposite. It means the hope of something better: the transformation of this sin-filled world. God gives us a longing for reconciliation, and that longing works toward healing. We become able to forgive as the longing for reconciliation grows stronger than any desire for separation or revenge. We forgive, finally, when love for God's reign wins out over hate for those who have wronged us.

Jesus' prayer from the cross means that even those who kill him can be accepted back into relationship with God. His prayer is for you and for me. If all of us could accept what Jesus holds out to the crucifiers from the cross, if we could all accept God's healing forgiveness and become reconciled with each other, with ourselves and with God, we would indeed enter the reign of God. For the kingdom of God is among us. Praying along with Jesus, in his suffering, for the

forgiveness of those who have injured us can help to make the reconciliation of all creation possible.

———————— §∾ ————————

Since that Good Friday over a year ago, I have moved far away
from my parents, and a new and happier phase of my life has begun.
Perhaps because of the safety of distance, perhaps because I am no
longer daily living out the most painful consequences of what my
father did to me, or perhaps simply because I am, for the most part,
satisfied with my life at last, I have made contact with both of my
parents for the first time in three years and permitted them to telephone me. Is this a new level of forgiveness? If so, it is a gift from
God. It feels like sorrow at being separated from my family, even
though I know that I cannot expect any more from them than in the
past. Perhaps this is the longing for reconciliation that I spoke about.
I have mixed feelings about our telephone conversation. I wish I
could say that we are miraculously reconciled, but that would not be
the truth. I told my parents that my husband and I might visit them at
some time in the future, and they seemed very pleased. They talked as
if they were grateful to hear from me and could not understand what
had gone wrong. If I visit them, I fear the resurgence of painful
feelings, of rage and hate, and the thought exhausts me. Perhaps this
stage in the road to forgiveness, or rather to possible reconciliation,
means, for me, being willing to risk exposing my feelings to my parents, not being prevented any longer by the fear of losing my sense of
the reality of the abuses I suffered.

My Good Friday analysis may have been a bit legalistic. I was
attached to the need for my father to admit what he did to me, and
perhaps I still am, because the fear of losing my sense of that reality
still crops up. But I trust that feelings work healing, whether the
feelings seem positive or negative, and I do not think I can be sure of
the final outcome. I trust LJ, my child-self, to keep me true to her
reality. Who knows, I might even feel reconciled with my parents
regardless of their denials one of these days, with God's help. Mean-

while, I try to remain open to the movements of the Spirit. I remind myself that I have the right to be true always to LJ, my child-self, and her feelings and perceptions of reality. I will not ever have to give up the reality of what happened to me in order to make reconciliation occur. I can trust God to work on reconciliation with my father; if he becomes reconciled with God, he will be reconciled with the truth, and with me. If I find myself at God's banquet and am asked to sit beside my father, I believe—I pray—that I will be willing to sit with him.

I have one more installment to add to the story of my attempt to forgive. I have left this as a run-on chapter to show the different stages in my struggle with forgiveness. Undoubtedly more stages will follow, after the publication of this book.

I found that my parents' failure to confirm my perceptions of my childhood reality and their failure to ask for my forgiveness made it very difficult to forgive them. They did not seem to want my forgiveness—forgiveness for what? And so I decided to take unilateral action. I wrote to them, listing in some detail all that I had been holding against them, and I told them that I forgave them for everything. After mailing the letter, I discovered that for me the crucial element of this attempt to forgive was the assertion of the truth. It meant testing and, at least for the moment, putting to rest my doubts. Beyond doubt, however, I faced guilt: What was I doing to my parents in asserting this truth? Old feelings of responsibility for them and the need to protect them flooded back. I felt that the truth was too cruel, that it would kill them. I wrote again and asked their forgiveness for hurting them, but I also asserted the necessity of doing so for my healing. I prayed for their healing too, but said that it must be their responsibility, not mine. They had, characteristically, failed to respond to the first letter, but now they responded, and they actually thanked me for forgiving them. They did not deny anything, but they also did not confirm anything. When their letter arrived, before I opened it, I found that not only guilt feelings remained; I experienced forcefully the old childhood fear of what they might do to me for speaking the truth. Their letter was a great relief, and I wrote and told them so.

The feeling that my assertion of truth might kill my parents brought to mind an early childhood dream in which a witch pointed a magic wand at my father to kill him. I knew that if I tried to warn him, she would kill me, but I felt I must try to save his life. I cried out, and the witch aimed her wand at me and killed me. Psychically, I paid the ultimate price to protect my father in childhood. Asserting the truth now meant reversing the dream, saving myself at what felt like his expense. I was actually killing him as an intrapsychic reality by finally rejecting his version of my childhood in favor of my own.

In the end, how can the truth hurt my parents? Satan is the prince of lies, and Jesus has promised that the truth will make us free. Jesus is, in fact, the light of truth, and he has told us that those who avoid his light judge themselves:

> And this is the judgment, that the light has come into the world, and men loved darkness rather than light, because their deeds were evil. For every one who does evil hates the light, and does not come to the light, lest his deeds should be exposed. But he who does what is true comes to the light, that it may be clearly seen that his deeds have been wrought in God (Jn 3:19–21).

I pray that my freedom will not be at my parents' expense. Fear and guilt linger on—and even doubt, from time to time—but the process of healing is well under way. To forgive is to be free of the past. To be free is to forgive.

Freedom comes when I am able to move beyond attitudes about the past to true relationship in the present. Hate is a feeling that, once fully experienced, passes away. An attitude of hate, not the feeling, ties us to the past and keeps us from forgiving, from being free. It is tempting to hang onto memories that were so difficult to discover and so necessary for healing, but nursing those memories can install hate. What we felt originally in reaction to abuse we continue to feel in response to thoughts about that abuse. Forgiving means no longer calling up memories, not needed anymore for healing, merely to perpetuate feelings of hatred and the desire for revenge.

Looking again at the process of forgiveness in myself, I can see that I continued to assert my "right" to hate my abuser because I had not learned to trust that my defensive aggressive feelings would arise spontaneously if I should ever again be abused, by my father or anyone else. I did not trust that, if I did feel anger or hate or pain, my feelings would count. I acted inwardly as if I had to keep anger and hate alive, or I would again be defenseless. In childhood I lost access to my aggressive feelings, and my feelings of pain and need carried no weight in relationships. But now that I have regained access to all my feelings I do not have to maintain consciousness of them; I will not lose them again, and I will not lose my ability to act on my feelings. I can defend myself. Therefore I can let go of the old memories and feelings. I can move beyond painful and aggressive feelings and per-ceptions from the past because I am free to feel and to perceive reality in the present. And I know now that I am a force in that reality, that I have an impact on others. For the first time, as I write this paragraph, I feel that I truly have forgiven my father.

CHAPTER 13

Toward True Relationship with Children

Many of the theological assertions in this book no doubt will raise questions about various child-rearing issues, including discipline. I aim primarily at dismantling harmful attitudes toward children, but I also hope that the practical implications of this theology of God the Child will become clear. When the inner healing of adults is well under way and we can trust who we are, with all our natural reactions, we will be able to trust ourselves to relate to children, and to each other, in life-giving ways.

I cannot offer a set of practical guidelines for child-rearing in accordance with this theology, both because, like Paul, I cannot codify the fruits of the Spirit, and because I write as a child, not as a child care expert, a parent, or an educator. I can, however, draw certain clues about the nature of true relationship with children from the foregoing explorations of the relationships of Mary and Joseph with Jesus, of God the Father with God the Child, and of the adult with the inner child-self. I will also refer to selected child care theory in exploring the meaning of true relationship with children, and, in Chapter 14, I will offer practical suggestions for the church.

As a child I can say to those who would rear me: "Treat me as Mary and Joseph must have treated Jesus. Enter into relationship with me and be guided by the divine Father-Child relationship revealed in the gospel. Take care of my needs. Give me structures and limits that let me know you care. Protect me from harm. Love me. Hold me. Value me. Let me know that I am your beloved daughter, that you are well pleased with me, and that you know I am worth listening to. Respect me and my feelings and my perceptions of reality. Do not have contempt for me. Do not lie to me. Do not use me or abuse me. Do not exercise power over me just to show me that you are the boss. Do not try to break my will or my spirit. Do not belittle my need for attention or my other needs. Teach me about the world and help me to learn about myself, but do not poison me with the belief that there is something evil or contemptible about me. Do not try to teach me how to be good, how to be God's child, or how to be me. Instead, through relationship with me, help me to know who and what I am. Recognize that only I can let you know who I am. Take a genuine interest in me, in how I feel and how I view things. Be yourself and let me be me. Trust me to grow into the human being God created me to be. If you feel helpless or enraged at times, pay attention to your feelings; they can help you to get in touch with your child-self and your own childhood experience. Do not expect perfection of yourself or of me.

"Above all, recognize that the result of the fall, the adult-child split, is in you, and try to heal the split in relationship with your child-self. Be ready to acknowledge when you are attributing your feelings to me or feeling feelings from your own childhood in relation to me. Let your child-self heal you and guide you. Relationship with your child-self can enable you to have empathy for me and for all children. Receive your child-self and receive me in the name of Christ, as God the Child incarnate, the new creation. Know that I am a creature in God's image. If you are in doubt about the way you are treating me in any situation, ask yourself if you would behave the same way toward the Child Jesus. Ask yourself if you would behave the same way if I were your age."

This book is related in many ways to my personal experience. The events of my life influence the ways I read the gospel and the meanings I derive from the relationships it portrays. Other children would draw different emphases in telling those who care for them what their needs are. Indeed, every child is an individual with unique needs, which adults can know only in relationship with that child.

Therefore, the ultimate child care rule is to relate to each child as an individual, letting relationship with the child keep you informed about her or his needs.

In speaking of moving beyond attitudes concerning good and evil in children, I do not mean to suggest an unrealistic appraisal of any individual child. Receiving a child as Christ does not mean think-ing that the child will always personify sweetness and light. The new creation includes everything the child is, with all feelings and all stages of development, including the "terrible twos" and adolescence.

Without a doubt, children do sometimes exhibit aggressive feel-ings and behavior. Children can feel anger, rage, and hate, and they can act out these feelings aggressively when they have no other way of experiencing and expressing their feelings and being heard. Often such feelings arise in reaction to adult contempt, abuse, or neglect.

In addition, children at certain stages of development naturally search for limits, and they need for their caregivers to set limits. Pediatrician and child care writer T. Berry Brazelton suggests that toddlers, for example, are naturally negative and provocative as they test their limits in the new world they are discovering. His experience tends to show that parents who can take this behavior in stride and set the necessary limits will avoid the power struggles that can only lead to aggressive reactions in children and increased frustrations for both parents and children.[1]

In a session with parents who had been unable to set limits for their daughter, who was in her second year, Brazelton helped the parents to see how their helpless reactions to their daughter's provoca-tive behavior served their own needs from their childhoods, not their daughter's needs.[2] Then,

> we were able to talk about Emily's needs—her need for contact with them and with their feelings, even their anger when she was negative and provocative. . . . We could talk about how an honest approach from them to her negative behavior would be reassur-ing, how limits for her provocative behavior would be felt by her

as love from them. She was searching for these limits, which make her feel loved and in contact with them.[3]

What the child seeks is "a real response."[4]

The temper tantrums and the testing episodes of the second and third years demand firmness, coupled with an understanding explanation to the child after the episode is over.[5]

The child needs the parents' real engagement, not evasions or mere management. The "limit setting" action that Brazelton suggests is holding and talking to the toddler, to show love, and, if that does not work, a cooling off time for the toddler in isolation, followed by reconciliation, discussion, and fun together.[6] The child's reaction to adult limit setting shows whether or not it has been effective. If it calms the child, it has "worked"; if it leads to aggression or further negativity or provocation, it has not helped but has made matters worse.[7] It is in such situations that parents are likely to experience their relationship with their child as a contest of wills and to feel that they need to break the child's will, when in fact the effort to do so will break the child's wholeness. Any confrontation with a child must show respect and not humiliate the child.

A mother of a slightly older child observed that when she remembered to acknowledge her son's anger and other feelings, he calmed down at once, while he became increasingly more agitated if she failed to take his feelings seriously. His reactions were markedly different in the two cases, even if her actions were otherwise the same. She could frustrate his wishes when necessary without unduly upsetting him if she took his reactive anger and disappointment seriously. Still, she found it very difficult to remember to do what was so simple, to say, "I know that you are angry and hurt, and I understand why you feel that way, but we cannot do what you want right now because (and give the reason). I am sorry." It so often seems easier to belittle the child's feelings, to make the child feel ashamed for having them. The same mother once observed: "Often you hear a parent say that she adores her child, but at the same time she does not trust his innate reactions; she thinks she has to teach him how to react appropriately."

Moving beyond attitudes to relationship with children means not only taking them and all their feelings seriously, but also letting their feelings have an impact on us. We cannot move beyond harmful attitudes, contempt and abuse until we can face the feelings of our own that we would prefer to avoid, which so often arise in reaction to the feelings and behavior of children. Originally we felt those feelings in reaction to our parents, who were larger and more powerful. Now we feel them in reaction to smaller and weaker beings, but we may react as if they were the more powerful ones. In fact, we are now strong enough not to be broken by the anger of the little ones. If we can avoid both contempt for the child's weakness and overestimation of the child's power, we will be secure in our adult roles and will not need to harm children. Allowing their feelings to open up our feelings can be healing for us.

It is important to experience our own power in relationships. We have to know what power we have before we can use it responsibly. A bully feels powerless and needs to prove that he or she has power by exercising power over others. A person who feels powerless feels justified in striking out at another. A person who cannot believe in her or his own power to injure another is a person who has not learned that she or he has a real impact on others. Knowing that we have power in relationships, power to hurt emotionally as well as physically, means knowing that we matter to others, that we really exist for them, that our feelings and behavior have a real impact on them.

Looking again at what Brazelton has to say about setting limits, the most important points, I believe, are that the child needs to feel "in contact" with the parents, that the child needs a "real response." In Chapter 10 I wrote of the human being in God's image as a sort of symbol of the divine. Relationship with the created truth in such a person leads us into relationship with God's truth. The created truth out of which we relate, and to which we relate in children, is not complete or perfect. We cannot measure this truth objectively, by some external standard. We can only know created truth subjectively, through experiences of relationship. Relationship out of our own created truth with the created truth in another human being is the truly life-giving relationship, the truly soul-nourishing relationship. The point of limit setting is not to make the child "good," but to be real in relationship with the child, to respond to what is really going on in the child, and thereby to enable the child to be real.

I am not a parent, but I have observed how young children sometimes tease and provoke their parents, seemingly asking for punishment. Can it be that children act in this way simply to be mean? Can they really want to be punished? Or can such behavior express a child's created truth? I believe it can. I began this work with the commitment to look at things from the children's point of view. If toddlers were able to observe themselves and to form concepts about their behavior, how would they make sense of actions that inevitably bring on parental wrath? I invite you to join me in this exploration.

Imagine that you have just arrived on a planet where everything is new and different from anything you have had contact with before. You want to discover all you can about your new environment. You use your senses to see, hear, taste, touch, and smell everything you can, within the limits of safety. You augment the effectiveness of your senses by using tools and instruments. You turn to reference books and computers to confirm what you can and to record what you are learning. If you meet living creatures, you attempt to make contact with them, to ascertain their level of intelligence, and what their intentions toward you are. Undoubtedly you feel many feelings in this process, such as excitement and fear. But your need to learn and your excitement in your discoveries overcome your fears. You need to explore the unknown, it may seem, at all costs.

A toddler too has a new planet to explore, but a toddler cannot use sophisticated tools and instruments or refer to books and computers to learn about the objects found there. A toddler's senses are the only tools available, and, having no idea of safety precautions, a toddler sets out to see, hear, touch, taste, and smell everything, from the kitchen stove to her or his own feces. There are other objects in a toddler's world, however, objects that are much more interesting than stoves. They are called adults. One day as a toddler discovers, say, an electric outlet, she or he discovers something else as well—a very interesting response from one of those adults: "Don't touch that!" This discovery arouses greater wonder than the others, because it also arouses feelings in the toddler. And it brings the adult and the toddler into direct contact with each other, their feelings engaged. For the moment, the adult's attention is focused on the toddler. The toddler enjoys the attention, and the adult's negative response is something for the toddler to imitate, a behavior to learn, while also learning about the adult. The toddler delights in these discoveries and learns how to behave in ways that will provoke more.

When we adults meet other adults, we too try to learn what we can: What kind of object (person) is this, anyway? We ask them questions about their work and their families. We may drop comments casually, just to see how they will respond. We choose what we will tell them about ourselves with a view to controlling our contact with them, while learning as much as possible about them. If they seem always to agree with us, we might push and tease, setting up contradictions to see if they will still agree. We want to know what they stand for, what they believe in. We want to know if they are the kind of people we can have meaningful contact with.

A toddler cannot resort to such subtleties, but uses a concrete approach. If touching an electric socket brings forth such interesting and real responses from an adult, then touching the electric socket becomes a much more interesting activity. Toddlers are just beginning to understand their own impact on reality, and in a sense adults' ultimate anger is a surprise every time. But this anger is not altogether unwelcome, because it too is real, and it helps a toddler gradually to gain a sense of the adult's and the toddler's own boundaries. As children mature, they begin to understand how their actions affect others and to generalize from experiences at home how other people are likely to react to certain kinds of behavior. They gradually learn how to get along as social beings.

The self-centeredness of very young children is unconscious. The testing episodes of adolescence extend those of early childhood to a new, self-conscious, emphasis on the effect the individual has on the environment. The way in which parents and other adults deal with limit setting in early childhood sets the scene for adolescence.

Children at every stage of development need real, firm, depend-able contact in order to develop a sense of boundaries and a sense of reality. If an adult who cares for a child is real and firm and depend-able and sets limits when necessary for the child's safety, or out of real, engaged feeling ("That's enough!"), the child will be able to know that the adult is real and that the child is real. The child will feel secure. We speak of being firm with children, and firmness should connote a real, solid quality, not punitiveness or severity. And in real relationship an adult never uses a child for sexual or any other purposes.

Alice Miller says that parents' freedom sets the necessary limits on a child's freedom.[8] I would add that the freedom of the parents that counts is the freedom to be who they are, to fulfill the created truth that constitutes the image of God in them. An adult whose personal boundaries are secure will not permit another person to tread on those boundaries, whether the other is an adult or a child. And such an adult will not need to be violent or punitive to keep those boundaries secure.

If children encounter nothing firm in their human environment, however, they will be confused, anxious, lacking boundaries, lacking a sense of reality. They will not be able to develop as solid, real, sane human beings. Returning to our exploration of another planet, imag-ine that the objects you examine do not behave predictably. Perhaps an object is sometimes firm to the touch and sometimes soft or fluid. You would react with confusion and, at some point, with anxiety. Going a step farther, imagine a world in which every object melts away before your touch. You sit down upon what appears to be a rock and fall to the ground because nothing solid is there. If even the ground fails to be solid, you float in space, unable to make real contact with any object on this elusive planet. Confusion and anxiety would quickly give way to terror, and ultimately your sanity would be at risk, as you would lose all sense of boundaries and thus of what is real. Toddlers too need objects that are solid, even if that solidity means opposition, so that they can know that the objects are real and that they are too. Adults are the most important objects in a toddler's environment in this regard. As toddlers discover adults, they begin also to discover themselves.

Adults can keep their angry reactions to children's limit-testing from getting out of control by keeping in mind that toddlers and adolescents are doing their appropriate developmental tasks when they test limits. If adults keep in mind the developmental appropriateness of provocative behavior and are not afraid to be firm, they need not take a child's behavior personally, lose control, or hurt the child either physically or emotionally. Remember that toddlers and astronauts have similar tasks of discovery; only their equipment is different. Children need limits, but they also need the freedom to explore within safe and reasonable bounds, to discover that Daddy is not the same as the stove, to learn about relationship with other human beings. It is the job of a child to test limits, just as it is the job of a parent to permit reasonable, safe testing and to set limits.

If adults artificially "control" their feelings, they may deny children the possibility of knowing what effect they have on others. Even a parent's anger, if it is genuine, is better than a parent's evasion or falseness. The truth and reality I speak of are known intuitively, and a child can tell when a response is genuine. If parents do not respond in a real way, the child will continue to push until the response is genuine, until it relates to the reality of the child. As the child pushes the parents for a real response, the child offers the parents the opportunity to find their own reality, to be reborn in the Spirit. In a sense the child's urgent need for truth, for real contact, thus sets limits for parents, helping them to find what is real in themselves.

Adults must, however, beware of the danger of discharging displaced anger onto children. Anger can be dangerous when it is loaded with feeling from the past. True relationship with a child can occur only when the adult's inner healing process is well under way, when the adult knows the source of her or his own aggression and is living in true relationship with the child-self. Then the "control" of feelings will be spontaneous, not a denial of reality. A person who is not whole cannot be real in relationship. Dangerous anger comes from brokenness; real (in terms of the present situation) and therefore safe

anger comes from wholeness. Toddlers "push" out of their develop-
ing wholeness, seeking a response from adult wholeness. They cannot
be held responsible for provoking the displaced rage that erupts from a
broken adult who is subject to the adult-child split.

Brokenness is untruth. The lie that breaks wholeness is: "I am
not a child. I am not small or weak. I do not feel anger, hate, or
humiliation." The lie takes over in childhood, splitting our wholeness, when our perceived reality is too horrible or too painful to
accept, when the contempt flowing from the brokenness of others
forces us into self-hate and brokenness.

We have all kinds of "reasons" for not being real in relationship
with others, with ourselves, and with our child-selves. We spend a lot
of time in relationships trying to decide what attitude we are going to
take, assuming that our feelings and actions will flow easily once we
have taken the "right" attitude. Our logical minds cannot help but
rationalize. When the real reason for intense feelings from the past is
hidden from consciousness, our minds search for reasons in the present: "If I feel this angry right now, it must be because of something
that is happening right now. You must be doing something to make
me so angry." Or, "It must be my fault, because I am a terrible person,
sinful, evil." Beneath such rationalizations is fear of knowing the
truth about the past, the child-self's reality. There cannot be a more
false relationship than the very denial of the other's (the child-self's)
existence. Until we are true to our inner reality, we cannot be real and
authentic in our relationships with others, including our children.

As a child whom I once knew was fond of saying, "Get real!" I
add to the parenting "rules" above: "Be real in relation to me, and let
me have an impact on you. You will be angry with me sometimes, and
I will be angry with you. Your anger is okay, as long as you do not act
it out in an abusive way or threaten me with the loss of your acceptance or love. Accept my anger and help me, by your way of dealing
with your own anger, to learn not to inflict my anger abusively on
others. Let us know together an anger that is not dangerous. Feelings
appropriate to the present situation will not harm you or me."

Not all the ways we can help children to know who and what
they are involve setting limits. Parents should emphasize the value of

the whole child. One of the ways we can come to know children and help them to feel real is in recognizing and appreciating their gifts. Every child has strengths and gifts as well as weaknesses and needs, and it is important to help a child to own her or his gifts, while also accepting and respecting the child's limitations and weaknesses. It may be most difficult to appreciate the ways in which limitations and weaknesses are themselves gifts.

Rejoice with your child in her or his strengths and gifts, but do not value the gifts more than you love and accept the child.[9] Remember that the gift is not something separate from the whole child. We can find ways to encourage a child's own wish to develop her or his gifts in the child's own way and own time, without exploiting the child. Genuine, empathic attention to a child's feelings will do more, for example, to help a child overcome a block against studying or practicing than laying down the law. A child who feels forced or manipulated will not be able to take genuine pleasure in an accomplishment, will never feel that it belongs to her or him, will never delight in it or own it. We must always remember that the gift belongs to the child and is ultimately the child's to use or not.

Real relationship, while it has the effect of letting other people know truths about themselves, also requires acknowledgment of a certain ignorance about who they are. New parents need to know about the care and development of babies, for example, but they should not imagine that they know in advance who their particular baby is. It is only possible to learn who a child is in relationship with the child. Truth emerges in both parent and child in the process of real relationship. In any relationship, we should never imagine that we have the other person pigeonholed; we are always in the process of coming to know him or her.

The same is true of ourselves—we come to know ourselves too in the process of relationship with ourselves, with others, and with God. We come to know ourselves and others, and help others to know themselves, in the process of real, engaged relationship, not by inquisitive, intrusive attention. We cannot gain this growing knowledge in a false relationship. When someone else tells us, you are this, or that, we can feel intuitively whether or not they are correct. It is the reality, the authenticity in others and in their way of relating to us that allows our own reality to unfold, that lets us feel real, behave authentically, be who we really are and know the feeling: "Yes, that is really me; you are real, and so am I."

As an adult I have discovered that my child-self has continued all my life to search for "limits." I have experienced the longing for limits as the wish to have a real impact on those I care about, to get a genuine response from them, and, at times, in emotional terms, to "land a solid punch." Aggressive acting out occurs when contact does not seem real. More than twenty years ago I overheard an acquaintance telling other friends how selfish and inconsiderate I had been on a sightseeing trip. I was surprised to discover that my embarrassment was slight in comparison to my sense of satisfaction in learning something real about myself. I had not realized that my behavior had any effect on those around me. I had not seen myself in that light, and the acquaintance's description of my behavior helped me to know myself better. The fact that he had observed me and spoken about me to others meant that I was real for him and for them. Did he set "limits" for me? I certainly was more aware of how my behavior affected others after that. For me, the "limit" was a consciousness of who I am and that I do have a reality and an impact in relation to others.

I have experienced more direct and more caring "limit-setting" since then, and I have found that each time I feel the thrill of knowing that I am real, that I really exist for another person, and that that person can perceive me as I really am. The sense of satisfaction is very deep as it gives to LJ, my child-self, what she missed in childhood, the experience of being real in relationship, of having an impact and receiving a response, of created truth meeting created truth in an encounter that speaks of God's Truth.

It is the contact with truth in another that actuates truth in a child. Without this real contact a child cannot know that she or he is real, or who she or he is. The important thing is a real response that relates accurately to what is real in a child, from the child's point of view. It is the responsibility of adults to help children to know who and what they are, not what adults think they ought to be. Parents and other adults can do this by observing children accurately, with empathy, and by relating to them with genuine feeling, out of wholeness.

The need for reality is one of our deepest needs, the very basis of our sanity and of our potential for any kind of satisfaction in life. To speak of "love" without the gift of truth is meaningless. Reality, inner truth, must be passed along from generation to generation. Without this truth shining forth from others, especially parents, onto a child, the child cannot know the child's own truth and reality.

Truth constitutes and institutes our spiritual nature. Spiritual growth begins as a search for truth; when we approach truth, we approach God, whether we expect to or not. Wholeness is nothing less than truth, the acceptance of inner and outer reality, however subjective our perceptions of those realities necessarily are. Healing comes from contact with wholeness. We yearn for this contact with other human beings. Whether or not we find it there, the search for truth may lead us to real relationship, real healing contact, with God.

CHAPTER 14

Words for the Church

My first inspiration to write this book came as I was reading the psychology of Alice Miller. Miller is very critical of the Judeo-Christian tradition for promoting the kind of authoritarian father model that I have addressed in Chapter 8.[1] Because I found so much of Miller's psychology personally helpful, I felt challenged to respond to her attack, to look at Christian traditions to find what is positive and healthful for the child.

Throughout its history the Roman Catholic Church has been strongly supportive of childbearing and family life. From its earliest times the church encouraged married couples to receive children willingly and struggled against pagan practices such as killing unwanted children or abandoning them to starve or to be killed by wild animals, or, if they were lucky, to be taken in (usually as slaves) by other families.[2] Theologies of the fall and original sin, together with the "spare the rod and spoil the child" theology of Proverbs and other scriptural and non-scriptural writings, however, encouraged the idea in some Roman Catholic and other churches' teachings that children must always obey adults and must be taught to be "good" and punished for their "evil" propensities. Thus the church, particularly at the local or popular level, has sometimes encouraged the formation of potentially harmful attitudes toward children rather than true relationship with them. Church teachings have failed to combat the human tendency, present due to the adult-child split, to have contempt for the smallness, weakness, and neediness of children. In its emphasis on obedience the church has fostered a power-based adult-child relationship rather than one based on mutuality and respect, like

136

the parent-child relationships revealed in the gospel (see Chapters 3 and 7). Thus I have found that Miller's accusations carry some weight. I trust that this book demonstrates, however, that the vast weight of true Christian belief is strongly on the side of the child.

In terms of a healing context, my writing relies not so much on Miller's psychology as on the very religion that Miller blames for its role in perpetuating harmful attitudes toward children. In fact, after nearly ten years of psychotherapy with three different therapists, I have reservations about the scientific model of individual therapy or analysis, at least insofar as it claims to provide an exclusive arena for emotional or psychic healing. The work of Miller and others shows that psychic and emotional ills (apart from those of genetic or bio-chemical origin) are manifestations of a sickness of family that is pervasive in our culture. I believe it is a symptom of our human brokenness, of our tendencies to fragmentation and isolation, that we identify the individual who suffers as the "sick" one, the one with the problems, and send that individual to a therapist or analyst to be "fixed." As suffering individuals we dutifully go to professional thera-pists or analysts, strangers who care nothing about us personally, to whom we pay large sums of money. If we are lucky we develop relationships with them in which we can feel sufficiently respected and cared for so that we can uncover the truth of our childhoods and be believed and supported in that discovery. But it is very difficult, if not impossible, for professionals who are themselves subject to the adult-child split to avoid identifying with our parents and urging reconciliation with them as a therapeutic goal.[3] On the other hand, I certainly do not blame the suffering individual who turns to psycho-therapy, often in desperation, because there seems to be no other place to turn. Family therapy often is not a realistic option, because other family members deny responsibility for what is wrong. Psychotherapy can be helpful to certain individuals in certain ways, but I question its ability to heal fully the adult-child split.

I believe it is true relationship, loving, respectful, real, support-ive relationship, that heals. What we need is healthy family in the broadest sense. Of course, since the sickness of our personal families caused our splits and repressions to begin with, we are not likely to find the healing relationships we need in our families. What my parents cannot give to me, however, they might be able to give to someone else, such as a grandchild or even someone unrelated to them. Someone else's parents might be able to do the same for me. I might even find "parents" among my contemporaries or among those younger than I, and I can similarly be healing "family" to persons outside my natural family. Marriage can be healing as spouses engage in true relationship with each other. In all these relationships, healing goes both ways; the one who facilitates healing also receives healing.

A younger priest has truly been father to me in a very deep and healing way. He not only accepted and believed me fully: he received every feeling, every experience I ever brought to him, no matter how horrible, as something of value, as part of the gift of who I am. Because of his unshakable integrity, I was able to love and trust him as a daughter ought to be able to love and trust her father, without fear of adult sexual complications or other forms of abuse. As a result, I discovered a sense of childhood purity and innocence prior to all abuse. I assure LJ, my child-self, that she will always retain this purity and innocence, and she in turn releases me from the need either to avoid my sexuality as an adult or to act out my sexuality in the role of an abuse victim. LJ's enduring purity and innocence are part of the foundation of my sense of self-worth.

The church should foster such healing relationships within the larger relationship that constitutes the heart of our faith. We should not contribute to fragmentation and brokenness within our society and its members. We should instead search for ways to enhance integration in community and in interpersonal relationships. In a healthy community, healthy families naturally will tend to emerge. I have been blessed by being a member of an accepting, healing parish community.

The church is the body of Christ, the Child incarnate. In the church, theologically based teachings that are health-producing for children can potentially reach a very broad audience, and true relationship with God and each other really can heal, much more fully than psychotherapy alone. There is more behind this theology than

practicality, however; truly Christian faith demands this kind of community and relationship.

There are many opportunities in the church for spreading the
good news of the unbroken Parent-Child relationship and its implications for parenting and teaching and healing. This theology can in-
form decisions concerning inclusive language, liturgy planning,
preaching, preparation for baptism and for marriage, the education of
parents, the training of those who teach or care for children, and, in
terms of healing the inner split, education, counseling, and spiritual
direction for persons of all ages. In attempting to make the language of
teaching and worship less sexist, parish staff could take care to point
out the healing and transforming significance of the gospel's Father-
Son relationship for human father- (or adult-) child relationships.
They could emphasize that the gospel portrays, not an authoritarian
Father, but one who relates to the Child and to us in mutuality,
respect, and wholeness. Worship in the Advent and Christmas sea-
sons should focus on the meaning of the good news that God is Child.
Christmas is the feast of children, and, in addition, at least two or
three Sunday homilies each year should address children's issues from
the children's point of view. Holy Family, for example, should not be
yet another occasion for telling children to be obedient, but a celebra-
tion of the good news of wholeness in family relationships, a reminder
to parents and to all adults to avoid contempt and to relate to children
as Mary and Joseph did, following the Father-Child model of the
gospel and remembering that each child received in the name of
Christ is Christ. Baptism preparation could include role-play exploring the feelings and attitudes of Mary and Joseph toward the child
Jesus, followed by discussion of the meaning of Jesus' annunciation
that each child received in the name of Christ is Christ. Similar
role-playing could be useful in parenting classes and teacher training
sessions. Participants might contrast what they discover about the
feelings and attitudes of Mary and Joseph with their own feelings and
attitudes about the children in their care. The good news of God the
Child and Jesus' annunciation could help them to bring disparate
views into a single focus. Those undertaking the counseling or spiri-

tual direction of adults could keep in mind the adult-child split and be aware of signs of contempt for weakness and neediness or of the attitude that any feelings are evil.

Parish staff and all community members should be particularly sensitive to the issues of child abuse, and parish education programs should train all who are interested to spot signs of abuse and to know what resources are available in the community for dealing with abusers, abuse victims, and their families. Clergy should let the community know from the pulpit that they are aware of the problem and are open to dealing with it. Parish staff should provide a clear channel for communication and action when abuse of any kind is suspected. All should remember that abuse does not happen only among the economically disadvantaged or minority groups (there is contempt again!), but across all social, economic, ethnic, and racial groups. It could happen in your neighbor's home; it could be happening in your home.

As examples of the kinds of teaching that can be done from the pulpit, addressed both to adults and to children, I include two reflections on scripture that I wrote as pastoral associate in charge of religious education for a large urban parish. I delivered the first as a homily to more than one hundred inner city children, ranging in age from six to seventeen, as part of a worship service during summer day camp. Many of the children were not Catholic, and some were not Christian. They all listened! I prepared the second, a longer written reflection, in connection with the gospel reading for Catechetical Sunday.

A Homily for Children
on Mark 10:13–16

And they were bringing children to him, that he might touch them; and the disciples rebuked them. But when Jesus saw it he was indignant, and said to them, "Let the children come to me, do not hinder them; for to such belongs the kingdom of God.

Truly, I say to you, whoever does not receive the kingdom of God
like a child shall not enter it." And he took them in his arms and
blessed them, laying his hands upon them (Mk 10:13–16).

Jesus and his disciples were surrounded by people. Some of the
people wanted to bring their children to Jesus so that he could touch
them. But the disciples didn't want to be bothered. You know how
sometimes adults don't seem to want to be bothered with children?
Well, the disciples didn't want to be bothered. There were lots of
grown-ups around, and the disciples thought they were more important than the children. And the disciples thought Jesus wouldn't
want to be bothered with children either. So they said, "Get away
from here with those children! Don't bother us!"

But the disciples were wrong. Jesus wanted to see the children
and touch them. Jesus wasn't bothered. Jesus said, "Let the children
come to me. Don't stop them! Let them come."

I read a story by a man called Kafka. Did any of you ever hear of
Kafka? Well, he wrote a story about this guy who lived with his
parents, and one morning he woke up and found that during the night
he had turned into a giant cockroach. Can you imagine, when his
parents opened his door in the morning, how they must have looked
at him? They expected to see their son, and there was this giant
cockroach! Imagine how they looked at him. Imagine how he felt. Do
you think his parents wanted to be bothered with him? They must
have looked at him like, "Yuch! Get away from us!" The way they
looked at him must have made him feel even worse than he already
did. Just think how it must have been for him. No one would touch
him. They left his food inside the door. They didn't want to spend
any time with him. They probably wished he had never been born.
The way they treated him, he would have felt like a cockroach even if
he hadn't already turned into one.

Well that's what the disciples were doing to those children.
They were making them feel like cockroaches by the way they looked
at them, the way they treated them. "Yuch! Get away from us! Don't
bother us."

Has anyone ever looked at you like you were a cockroach? Do

you know what I mean? Some of you may think that I have looked at you like you were a cockroach. And maybe I have; maybe I have. I can guarantee you that right now some of you are looking at me like I'm a cockroach. And I know that the reason you are looking at me that way is because someone else has looked at you that way.

Well, when the disciples started making the children feel like cockroaches, do you know what Jesus did? He let them know that he doesn't look at children that way.

To you Jesus says, "I love you!"

Jesus says, "I want to spend time with you!"

Jesus says, "I'm glad you were born!"

Jesus says, "Come to me! I'm glad you were born! I want to touch you. I want to spend time with you! I love you!"

Not only that, but Jesus actually thinks that children are more important than adults. Jesus says that his kingdom, the kingdom of God, belongs to the children! He says that if adults don't become like children, they will never get into the kingdom!

[Showing a figure of the Infant of Prague] This is a figure of the child Jesus. He is a child, and he is king! Jesus is saying that his kingdom belongs to every one of you too. Jesus shares his crown with you. Each one of you is king! [I hold up a crown] I can't put this crown on every one of you today, but I think I'll put it on one of you, to show that all of you are kings. [There are several volunteers—one emerges; I look straight into his eyes and carefully place the crown on his head, saying] "You are the king!" Jesus says to every one of you, "You are the king!"

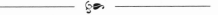

The child wore the crown until the end of the worship service, and then he brought it back to me. The children had some free time before their next activity, and one after the other they came to me to be crowned. Their faces were filled with joy. One little boy took the crown off his own head and put it on mine, saying, "You are the king." The girls seemed more reluctant than the boys to come for- ward, so I approached them. They felt that as girls they could not be "king." I told them that they could, that the kingdom is for every-body, that girls share Jesus' kingship just as much as boys do. They were delighted. Even the toughest of this tough crowd responded. The children seemed to form a community for the first time during the summer camp.

"Yielding to Chaos"
Reflections on Mark 9:30–37

They went on from there and passed through Galilee. And he would not have any one know it; for he was teaching his disci-ples, saying to them; "The Son of man will be delivered into the hands of men, and they will kill him; and when he is killed, after three days he will rise." But they did not understand the saying, and they were afraid to ask him.

And they came to Capernaum; and when he was in the house he asked them, "What were you discussing on the way?" But they were silent; for on the way they had discussed with one another who was the greatest. And he sat down and called the twelve; and he said to them, "If any one would be first, he must be last of all and servant of all." And he took a child, and put him in the midst of them; and taking him in his arms, he said to them, 'Whoever receives one such child in my name receives me; and whoever receives me, receives not me but him who sent me" (Mk 9:30–37).

Chapter 9 of Mark is a chapter that has a lot to do with children. It begins with the transfiguration, in which God reveals that Jesus is his "beloved Son" and says, "Listen to him." Jesus is the Son who speaks, and the Father has faith in his Son and tells Peter, James, and John to listen to him. Then they go down from the mountain and find the other disciples trying to cast out a dumb spirit from a boy, a son who cannot speak. And he cannot be made whole because his father does not have faith, in his own son or in the Son, Jesus. When the father admits his lack of belief and asks Jesus for help, Jesus casts out the spirit. Now this son too can speak, and his father must listen to him. Children are to be heard as well as seen!

Now we find Jesus and the disciples on the road in Galilee. Jesus tries to tell the disciples that he will be killed and that after three days he will rise again. But the disciples are unable to listen to this. To them, death is a manifestation of chaos, the opposite of creation. If Jesus is the Creator's Son, how can he die? They envision worldly dominion for Jesus.

They continue walking, discussing which of them is the great-est—they really haven't gotten the message at all. Jesus knows this, and tries yet again, telling them that anyone who wants to be first must be last and must be the servant of all. And Jesus' example of one whom they must serve is a child. If anyone receives a child in Jesus' name, she or he receives Jesus, the Christ, God the Child incarnate.

God the Father has faith in the Son. Fathers must have faith in their children if their children are to be whole. Jesus says that the child is Christ, if we have faith, if we receive the child in Christ's name. And, as Christians, how else can we receive them?

But how often do we receive a child as Christ? How often do we have faith in the child? How often do we listen to our children? We are more likely to receive the children as the disciples received Jesus' prediction that he would be killed: Chaos!

I was talking recently with two couples in the parish. One cou-ple has two children, and the other couple were talking about their anticipation of having children. The couple with children said that when a child arrived, they lost control of their lives. There was no more time for anything. Old pastimes went out the window. Even career decisions had to be subordinated to the exigencies of child-rear-ing, especially in the case of the mother. Their lives were turned upside down. They love their children very much and would not give them up for anything, but "chaos" was not too strong a word for what children brought to their lives, much of the time.

The second couple eagerly await the time when they will be parents. But they are aware, at least as aware as people can be before chaos actually strikes, that having children will affect their lives enor-mously. The prospective mother has a demanding career, and she wonders whether she will be able to continue it with a child. Both are uncertain about remaining in this city long-term, and children probably will affect decisions about where they will live and what sort of housing they will be able to afford. They have some sense of losing control of their lives, of facing impending chaos.

And how do we as a worshiping community feel when the children come in from the children's liturgy of the word on Sunday mornings and join us for the eucharist? How do we feel about small children who stay with their parents through the whole mass, sometimes crying or running around? Do we receive each of them as Christ? Or do we have the sense that things are getting out of control, a bit too chaotic?

I would like to suggest that a little chaos is not necessarily a bad thing. Ancient Israelites saw God in the most chaotic of natural phenomena, the earthquake. And later the Jews saw in chaotic events in nature and history the apocalyptic signs of God's imminent coming. As Psalm 139 tells us, even in Sheol, God is there.

What would happen if we decided to yield to chaos? The disciples couldn't bring themselves to yield to the chaos of Jesus' impending death. But he died anyway. Adults sometimes have a hard time accepting the chaos that children bring to their lives. But they bring it anyway. Good parenting, in fact, must include the ability to accept a little chaos in one's life. We like to think that we can control everything, but we can't. We aren't meant to. And children make this abundantly clear. Children even show us that we cannot always control our feelings. Children reveal to us our chaos on the inside, our fears and other feelings that we usually don't want to face.

As an adult, I have learned from experience the profound difficulty of facing what feels like impending chaos. I believed that I had great empathy for the suffering of any person who was treated unfairly, hurt, or rejected. In personal relationship with children, however, I have discovered that what I experienced was not empathy, but identification. Being in touch with certain painful feelings, I identified with those who seemed to suffer the same feelings. In trying to deal empathically with children whose wholeness had been broken by contempt and possibly by abuse, however, I found that in reaction to their discharge of displaced reactive aggression I felt that I was their victim. Their aggression—or "misbehavior" (i.e. their failure to submit to my efforts to keep them "under control")—broke my identification with them as "victims" and dispelled any semblance of empathy. I quickly fell into a destructive "us or them" mentality. This experience brought home to me the profound difficulty of facing chaos creatively in order to break the cycle of contempt and abuse. I could see that my increasing agitation and need to control increased the children's agitation and "misbehavior" as well, thus accelerating a vicious circle. Only my conscious recognition of what was going on—not any effort to control them—could calm me or the children. When I calmed down, so did they.

I know from experience the feeling of helplessness and the outbursts of controlling behavior that crop up in us adults in relation to many children. My effort when this occurs is to try to figure out not what to do about them, but what to do about me. I must turn again to my child-self for instruction and healing. Meanwhile, perhaps there will be some chaos. I am not convinced that chaos, accompanied by honesty, will be any more harmful than following the urge to control and manipulate, discharging my own displaced childhood aggression onto the children for the sake of order—an adult purpose.

When working with children makes me feel I cannot do anything right, I can recall that they are unconsciously telling me how they have been made to feel. At the same time they are arousing in me feelings that I too was made to feel as a child. The adult learning process may be slow, and messy, and, like all movements of the Spirit, we cannot be certain of its outcome. We can only be certain that the child-rearing path we have followed up to now is a pathway (if not, perhaps, the only pathway) to inner splits and repressions, and to oppression and violence in the world. Living out the theology of the Child would not, however, mean an end to pain or to conflict between parents and children, but a radical restructuring of relationships giving new possibilities for dealing with unavoidable pain and conflict in ways that do not oppress others or increase pain and conflict.

As I said before, the disciples saw chaos as the opposite of creation. Before creation, there was chaos. To them chaos was un-creation, and therefore evil. But there is another way of looking at chaos. Chaos was the raw material out of which God created the heavens and the earth. And chaos in our lives too can be creative, if we yield a little and give God a chance once again to be creative in the midst of chaos, to do some new creative work in our lives. After all, God creates the child who brings chaos into our lives and into our worship. And Jesus says that if we receive the child in his name, we receive him, we receive God the Child incarnate.

In fact, doesn't Jesus himself, God the Child, bring chaos into our lives? We would like for conversion to be nice and neat and under control—our control, that is. But often conversion, faith in Christ, turns our lives upside down. A comfortable Wall Street lawyer finds herself going to seminary and becoming Roman Catholic. What could be more chaotic than that? Yet in our lives yielding to chaos may indeed fulfill the apocalyptic expectation and instate the new creation. The apparent chaos gives way to a new sense and order in our lives.

Receiving children in Christ's name, accepting the chaos, even embracing it, can be a sort of spiritual discipline. It means yielding one's life to greater necessities than keeping things tidy and rational. It means letting life itself, new life in the child, come first. It means having faith in the child, and in God, the child's Creator. The child truly does bring God's truth to us. The child is Christ among us. It means saying of every child, "This is my beloved son or daughter. Listen to him. Listen to her."

Today is Catechetical Sunday. Perhaps part of the meaning of this passage from Mark is that receiving children in Christ's name is catechesis for us adults. Receiving with joy the chaos they bring may help us to do what the disciples could not do, to hear the prediction of Jesus' passion as good news, and to hear God's call in our own lives as good news, whether it is a call to parenthood, or to teach CCD, or to have children sit near us at mass.

As far as the catechesis of children is concerned, the key is, really, how we receive them. How we receive children teaches them more about faith than any number of lessons. We must receive them as the Father received the Son, and as Jesus received the children. Receive them into relationship with us. Have faith in them and know that they are worth listening to. They will learn far more about loving, caring for, and valuing others if we love them, care for them and value them, than if we tell them any number of stories about loving, caring, and valuing. It is not possible to teach anyone to be good. We can only relate to the good that is in them, the good that is God's creation and God's gift.

"Why Are You Afraid? Have You No Faith?"
(Mk 4:40)

Giving up contempt and attitudes about the good and evil of children may seem impossible—like calming a storm, or moving a mountain, or getting a camel through the eye of a needle. But as Jesus said of the rich young man's plight, "With men it is impossible, but not with God; for all things are possible with God"(Mk 10:27). The problem, as Jesus so often reminded us, is that we lack faith. Overcoming contempt, healing our adult-child splits, and being able to leave children in their wholeness, free to be whoever and whatever God created them to be, all require faith.

What radical faith it takes to trust in the natural development of your child as you would trust a mustard seed to grow into a plant! Have faith as a grain of mustard seed itself has, and the child, your child and the child-self within you, will grow as God intends. Faith means faith in God, in God's gift of goodness in creation, in each other as creatures in God's image. This faith necessarily implies corrected relationship with ourselves (the child within) and each other (the child without), as well as with God. Faith means recovered wholeness, the reign of God in our midst, which we receive as little children or not at all.

Our lack of faith means that we do not take the new creation seriously. We say that the life, death, and resurrection of Jesus, the Christ, have changed everything, that the new creation is "already" realized, but our attitudes toward creation and especially toward children reveal that we do not really believe that anything has changed. We look around at the state of our world, at children themselves, and we seem to see proof that nothing has changed. Does the lack of visible change simply expose that we are in fact evil, or a mixture of good and evil, and that no real change is possible until the eschaton? If so, then where is our faith? What is the point of the incarnation if not to announce and effect a real transformation "in our midst"?

Nothing prevents us from fulfilling the promise of the new creation except our unbelief. Our unbelief holds us in the "not yet." Every child is a new creation who can be allowed to live for the new, or because of our brokenness and lack of faith be dragged back into the old. Every one of us is in his or her child-self a new creation waiting to be fulfilled, made whole. If we can overcome our fear and our lack of faith and live in true relationship with our child-selves and with children, the reign of God may appear right before our eyes. What we find out about the nature of children in the process of true relationship with them may be quite different from what we have experienced in the past, in relationships distorted through our attitudes about children.

In Mark 9:14ff., Jesus could cause a deaf and dumb spirit to leave a man's child only if the child's father believed. Acknowledging his unbelief and asking for help, the father freed his son to be healed by the Son. That father's cry can guide us in our search for faith and wholeness: "I believe; help my unbelief!"

Remember that the child, every child, is Christ for you. There is no need to be afraid.

Notes

Introduction

1. Robert McAfee Brown, *Creative Dislocation—The Movement of Grace* (Nashville: Abingdon, 1980) 127.

2. Ibid.

Chapter 1

1. Alice Miller, *Prisoners of Childhood,* trans. by Ruth Ward (New York: Basic Books, Inc., 1981) 65–66 (hereinafter cited as Miller, 1981).

I am greatly indebted to the ideas of Alice Miller throughout this book. In a sense, this book is a response to Miller's criticism of Christian tradition for its role in causing child abuse. See her books, *For Your Own Good,* trans. by Hildegarde and Hunter Hannum (New York: Farrar, Straus & Giroux, Inc., 1983) (hereinafter cited as Miller, 1983), and *Thou Shalt Not Be Aware,* trans. by Hildegarde and Hunter Hannum (New York: New American Library, 1986) (hereinafter cited as Miller, 1986).

2. Miller, 1981, 66.

3. Ibid. 66–67.

4. Biblical quotations are from Herbert G. May and Bruce M. Metzger, eds., *The Holy Bible, Revised Standard Version* (New York: Oxford University Press, 1973). While I prefer an inclusive language lectionary in many contexts, for purposes of this book I have usually retained the RSV's masculine usage.

Chapter 2

1. See generally Miller, 1983.
2. Miller, 1986, 156, 209, 306.
3. Brown, 127.

Chapter 3

1. Miller, 1983.
2. Ann Belford Ulanov, Final Course Evaluation for M. Div. Thesis, "Toward a Theology for the Liberation of Children: A Theological Exploration in Light of the Psychology of Alice Miller," May 4, 1988.

Chapter 4

1. David H. Kelsey, "Human Being," *Christian Theology,* Peter Hodgson and Robert King, eds. (Philadelphia: Fortress Press, 1985) 177.
2. Robert R. Williams, "Sin and Evil," *Christian Theology,* Peter Hodgson and Robert King, eds. (Philadelphia: Fortress Press, 1985) 217–219.
3. Hubert Benoit, *The Supreme Doctrine* (New York: Viking Press, 1955) 213–215; cf. 6–14 (" 'Good' and 'Evil' ").
4. Miller, 1983, 232, 249, 272; Miller, 1986, 96, 192. Cf. Benjamin Spock, M.D., and Michael Rothenberg, M.D., *Baby and Child Care* (New York: Pocket Books, 1985) 9; D.W. Winnicott, *The Maturational Processes and the Facilitating Environment* (New York: International Universities Press, Inc., 1965) 94.
5. Charles R. Swindoll, *You and Your Child* (New York: Bantam Books, 1977) 22.

Chapter 5

1. Swindoll, 22. Swindoll also acknowledges a "bent toward good" in the child. Ibid. 17.

2. Ibid. 22.

3. Ibid. 24.

4. Ibid. 94.

5. Ibid. 98.

6. Ibid. 86.

7. Augustine of Hippo, *Confessions,* trans. by R.S. Pine-Coffin (Harmondsworth, England: Penguin Books, 1961) 27.

8. Miller, 1983, 58, 61, 91, 97–99; Miller, 1986, 156.

9. Miller, 1986, 156.

10. Augustine, 25, 27.

Chapter 6

1. Quoted in Miller, 1986, 218. Miller notes that the last four words of the quotation have been omitted from most translations of Freud's works, including the official translation.

2. Miller, 1986, 156, 200ff.

3. See, e.g., Miller, 1983; Winnicott (more evident in reports of therapeutic practice than in theoretical writings); Harry Guntrip, *Psychoanalytic Theory, Therapy, and the Self* (New York: Basic Books, Inc., 1973) 137; Heinz Kohut, *The Analysis of the Self* (Madison, Conn.: International Universities Press, Inc., 1971).

4. Miller, 1983, 64.

5. Miller, 1986, 195–197.

6. Miller, 1986, 148.

7. Miller, 1986.

8. Thomas Merton, *Faith and Violence* (Notre Dame: University Press, 1968) 8.

9. Ibid. 10.

Chapter 7

1. G. Schrenk and G. Quell, "πατήρ," (or "patēr,") *The Theological Dictionary of the New Testament,* Vol. 5 (1964) 984–985.

2. Ibid. 985.

3. Ibid. 984–985.
4. Miller, 1983, 180.

Chapter 8

1. E.g., Jaroslav Pelikan, ed., "Lectures on Galatians, 1535," *Luther's Works,* Vol. 26, chap. 1–4 (St. Louis: Concordia Publishing House, 1963) 416 (quoted at text accompanying note 12 to this chapter).

2. Miller, 1983, 44–45 (quoting K.A. Schmid, ed., *Enzyklopädie des gesamten Erziehungs und Unterrichtswesens* [A Comprehensive Encyclopedia of Education and Instruction], 1887).

Miller took the quotations cited in notes 2–4 to this chapter from Katharina Rutschky, *Schwarze Pädagogik* (Black Pedagogy) (Berlin, 1977).

3. Miller, 1983, 28–29 (quoting Schmid).
4. Miller, 1983, 39–40 (quoting L. Kellner, 1852).
5. Augustine, 30.
6. Ibid.
7. Pelikan, 235.
8. Ibid.
9. Ibid. 58, 174.
10. Ibid. 186.
11. Ibid. 188.
12. Ibid. 416.

Chapter 9

1. Schrenk and Quell, 970, 978. See chapter 10, note 16, and accompanying text.

2. Miller says that the original anger is the child's anger in reaction to the narcissistic, emotional, physical, and other wounds inflicted in a pedagogical upbringing—one designed to make the child "good." Adult anger toward those the adult perceives as weaker, such as children, is a discharge onto the projected split-off weaker part of the self of repressed anger displaced from the adult's own childhood experience of authoritarian, or even "antiauthoritarian," pedagogy. Miller, 1986, 60–61, 150. (It seems to me

that a pedagogy designed to teach a child not to respect authority is itself an imposition of authority and thus "authoritarian" in another guise.)

3. Richard Norris, *Understanding the Faith of the Church* (New York: Seabury Press, 1979) 78.

4. Cf. Miller, 1986, 175 (Hitler is Miller's example).

5. See Miller, 1983, 115, 177.

6. In terms of the theory of narcissism, it is the child who has the right to use the parent as a self-object. Instead, the child is used as a substitute for the self-object that the parent, in his or her own childhood, lacked. Miller, 1986, 123, 241.

7. Cf. Winnicott, 96.

Chapter 10

1. Paul Ricoeur, *Freud and Philosophy: An Essay on Interpretation*, trans. by Denis Savage (New Haven: Yale University Press, 1970) 15ff, 29.

2. Ibid. 16.

3. Ibid. 539; see also 543.

4. Ibid. 240, 533, 537.

5. Ibid. 530–531.

6. Ibid. 32ff, 530–531, 543.

7. Ibid. 539.

8. Ibid. 29.

9. Ibid. 534ff, 541–542.

10. See Miller, 1986, 93–96, 219.

11. See Miller, 1983, 3–63; chapter 8, notes 2–4 and accompanying text.

12. See generally Miller, 1983; see Miller, 1983, 96, 150.

13. E.g., Ann Belford Ulanov, "Picturing God," *Picturing God* (U.S.A.: Cowley Publications, 1986) 172.

14. Ulanov, 167.

15. Ricoeur, 32ff, 530–531, 543.

16. Schrenk and Quell, 973; cf. Jeremiah 3:19; but see Isaiah 63:15–16; 64:8.

17. Schrenk and Quell, 996–997.

18. See Schrenk and Quell, 988, 998.

19. Cf. Schrenk and Quell, 978, 980, 999.

20. See Norris, 102.
21. Ricoeur, 534ff, 541–542.
22. Miller, 1986, 200ff.

Chapter 11

1. See, e.g., Winnicott; Guntrip; Kohut; and Miller, 1986, 190–191. Miller, however, also addresses the child as a whole within the adult, and she speaks of the splitting off of "the vital child within." Miller, 1983, 117.
2. See Norris, 100f.
3. Roland Bainton, *Here I Stand* (New York: Abingdon-Cokesbury Press, 1950) 302.
4. Miller, 1983, 87, 98, 223, 242.
5. See generally Miller, 1983; Miller, 1986.
6. See Miller, 1983, 87, 98, 223, 242.
7. See Miller, 1986, 299; Winnicott, 96.
8. See Winnicott, 54; D. W. Winnicott, *The Family and Individual Development* (New York: Basic Books, 1965) 3.

Chapter 12

1. Schrenk and Quell, 965.
2. Miller, 1983, 17, 64, 144, 242.
3. Miller, 1986, 317–318. See also Miller, 1983, 263.
4. Miller, 1983, 247–248.
5. Miller says that healing means mourning a past that cannot ever be changed and that therapy is not a corrective emotional experience. Ibid. 100, 177, 250, 270, 273; Miller, 1986, 52, 55, 183, 207. Miller also says, however, that acknowledging unmet needs can help to develop "an empathic inner object." Miller, 1986, 300.

Chapter 13

1. T. Berry Brazelton, M.D., *To Listen to a Child* (Reading, Mass.: Addison-Wesley Publishing Company, 1984) 87–89.

2. Ibid. 85.
3. Ibid.
4. Ibid. 87.
5. Ibid. 88.
6. Ibid. 84, 88.
7. Ibid. 82, 88.
8. Miller, 1983, 98.
9. See generally Miller, 1981. Miller describes her discovery and development of her child-self's artistic gifts in adulthood in Alice Miller, *Pictures of a Childhood,* trans. by Hildegarde Hannum (New York: Farrar, Straus & Giroux, Inc., 1986).

Chapter 14

1. See Miller, 1983, 64, 116–118, 144, 242; Miller 1986, 93, 94, 99, 156, 201, 209, 219, 306.
2. Lloyd de Mause, "The Evolution of Childhood," *The History of Childhood: The Untold Story of Child Abuse,* Lloyd de Mause, ed. (New York: Peter Bedrick Books, 1974) 28; Richard B. Lyman, Jr., "Barbarism and Religion: Late Roman and Early Medieval Childhood," Ibid. 90. The de Mause book is excellent in general for psychological, social, and historical analyses of child abuse.
3. Miller rejects reconciliation with parents as a therapeutic goal. Miller, 1983, 252–253; Miller, 1986, 14, 183, 204–205.

Index

abandonment, 7, 12, 19, 48, 60, 101, 136

Abba or Dada, 58ff., 63, 84–85, 100, 111, 113

abuse, 14, 16–17, 20, 23, 25, 34, 37, 40, 44, 48ff., 57, 59ff., 63, 65, 69–70, 71, 73, 76, 79, 88–89, 91–92, 95, 98, 101, 106, 108, 110ff., 116, 119, 121, 124–125, 127, 132, 138, 140, 145; consequences of, 1, 64, 100, 107, 109, 111, 119; cycle of, 22, 63, 103, 108, 146; emotional or psychological, 1, 3, 5, 7, 10ff., 25, 43, 67ff., 72, 100, 108, 110, 127, 131, 133, 146; physical, 1, 3, 5, 7, 10, 41ff., 54, 64ff., 72, 100, 108, 127, 131, 133, 136; religious rationalizations for, 2, 30, 41, 58, 66; sexual, 1, 5, 7, 10, 19, 47, 49ff., 57, 95, 100, 108, 114, 116, 130, 138; victims of, 1, 2, 5, 18, 20–21, 45, 51ff., 96ff., 106, 138, 140; need of for understanding and support, 49, 51, 137; tendency of to abuse, 1, 5, 7, 17–18, 20, 54–55

abuser, 15, 27, 41, 47ff., 51ff., 91, 96, 108, 116, 122, 140

acceptance, 89, 97, 111, 113, 117, 132ff., 138

acting out, 45, 54, 92, 110, 125, 132, 134, 138

action, 17, 45, 48, 53–54, 91, 109, 120, 132, 140

Adam, 26, 31, 32, 34, 37, 67

adolescence, 6, 7, 125, 129, 131

adult-child split, 2, 3, 9–10, 18–19, 26–27, 40, 61–62, 64–65, 70, 75, 76–77, 79, 81–82, 83–84, 88, 91, 94, 98, 103, 105, 111–112, 124, 132, 136–137, 140, 148; *see also* split

adultist assumptions, 15

aggression or aggressive feelings, 3, 16, 29, 43ff., 47–48, 51, 69, 73, 78, 95–96, 105, 107, 110, 122, 125–126, 131, 134; reactive, 3, 30, 41, 48,

Index of Biblical References